Longman Test Practice Kits

Mathematics

Key Stage 3

Brian Speed

Longman

Series editors
Geoff Black and Stuart Wall

Titles available
Key Stage 2
English
Mathematics
Science

Key Stage 3
English
Mathematics
Science

Addison Wesley Longman Ltd.,
Edinburgh Gate, Harlow,
CM20 2JE England
and Associated Companies throughout the World

First Published 1998

ISBN 0582 31572-7

British Library Cataloguing-in-Publication Data
A catalogue record for this book is available from the British Library.

Set by 32 in 10.5/16pt Frutiger light
Produced by Longman Singapore Publishers Pte.
Printed in Singapore

Table of contents

The Key Stage 3 National Tests 1
How they work 1
Levels of achievement 1
Levels of entry (tiers) 2

Using this book 3
Mathematics at Key Stage 3 3
Part 1 Self-check revision 3
Part 2 Test practice papers 3

Part 1 **Self-check revision 4**
Revision progress chart 4
Topics 1–6 7
Answers to self-check questions 37

Part 2 **Test practice papers 38**
Taking practice tests 38
Marking the questions 38
Test A 39
Test B 61
Answers to Test A 82
Answers to Test B 87

The Key Stage 3 National Tests

How they work

During the years 7–9 your child will be studying Mathematics, Science and English as part of Key Stage 3 of the National Curriculum. At the end of Year 9 (at age 14) your child will take National Tests in each of these subjects.

These written National Tests (sometimes called SATS) will take place in May of Year 9. The tests are taken in your child's own school, but they will be marked by examiners from outside the school.

There will be two written exam papers for Mathematics, one to be taken without a calculator, and the other with a calculator available. Each exam is 1 hour long. Your child will also take a mental arithmetic test which lasts for 20 minutes.

You will receive the results of your child's National Test by the end of July. Along with these Test results, you will receive the results of assessments made by your child's teacher in the classroom.

You will find that your child's results are expressed as a Level for both the National Test and the teacher assessment.

You will also receive a summary of the Key Stage 3 results achieved by all the other students in your child's school, and for all students nationally. You will then be able to check your child's progress against other students of their age.

Levels of achievement

Each subject is divided into Levels 1–8 at Key Stage 3. The table below illustrates what percentage of students, nationally, are expected to gain each Level. You can see from the table that the average student is expected to reach Level 5 by the end of Key Stage 3.

Percentages of students reaching a particular Level in Mathematics

Level	Percentage
1	0
2	2
3	12
4	24
5	26
6	25
7	10
8	1

Levels of entry (tiers)

Different National Test papers are set for students of different ranges of ability. For Mathematics, your child will be entered for one of the four possible tiers from:

Level 3–5
Level 4–6
Level 5–7
Level 6–8

Your child's teachers will decide which tier they should be entered for. Each tier is examined by two written test papers, both lasting 1 hour, and a mental arithmetic test lasting 20 minutes. (There are also Extension Test Papers for the exceptionally able students, covering questions set at Level 8 and above.)

This book concentrates on Levels 4–7 and presents questions of the type your child can expect to face in the actual examination.

The Level of the work is shown in capitals next to each topic heading or subheading. Make sure your child knows which paper they are being entered for so that they are not trying to cover topics that they will not have been taught yet.

Similarly, the test papers indicate which Level the questions are being aimed at. Your child should not attempt the questions from a Level way above their own. Your child should try to concentrate on what they have already been taught to do and on the material set at the appropriate Level.

When your child tries the papers please remember that they should *not* use a calculator for the *non*-calculator papers.

Using this book

Mathematics at Key Stage 3

In order to assess Mathematics, the National Curriculum divides Mathematics into four sections, called Attainment Targets (ATs).

AT1   Using and Applying Mathematics
AT2   Number and Algebra
AT3   Shape, Space and Measures
AT4   Handling Data

AT2, AT3 and AT4 are examined in the National Tests. Your teacher will assess AT1.

Part 1 Self-check revision

Part 1 (pages 4–37) of this book gives a brief outline of the six key topics that your child should know for the Key Stage 3 Test in Mathematics. Your child should work through Part 1 *before* trying the actual tests in Part 2 of this book. We have tried to make this book more interesting by asking your child to fill in blanks in the text using words or calculations, as appropriate. Doing this will help your child to check their knowledge and understanding of the topic being studied. Answers to all the blank spaces can be found at the end of Part 1 (page 37). On pages 4–6 there is a Revision Progress Chart; tick the topic when your child has revised and understood the topic completely. If you feel your child needs more information on a topic you could always use the *Longman Homework Handbook Key Stage 3 Mathematics.*

Part 2 Test practice papers

Part 2 contains the following:
- **Questions**   Two full test practice papers, one covering Levels 3–5, the other covering Levels 6–8. Each paper contains two separate one-hour examinations, one to be answered with a calculator, the other without a calculator.
- **Answers and mark scheme**   Full solutions to all the questions, with breakdown of marks awarded, and a reference guide to Part 1 if you need more information. As a parent, you should take responsibility for marking the tests in this book.
- **Examiner's tips**   Helpful advice from an examiner to help you to improve your child's score.
- **Marking grid and Level chart**   A guide to the marks needed to achieve each Level.

PART 1

Self-check revision

In this part of the book you will find a brief, easy-to-use review of the topics and techniques you are expected to know for your National Test. The six topics selected cover the three Attainment Targets (ATs) outlined on page 3 as being the focus of the National Test. To help make your revision more active and interesting, you will find a series of questions, in the form of blank spaces to be filled in, set on each of the six topic areas. **Answers to all these questions can be found at the end of Part 1 (page 37).**

After you have revised a topic, and completed the questions set on that topic, place a tick in the appropriate box in the Revision Progress Chart below. This will help you to keep a record of your progress. It will be best if you revise all six topics *before* you attempt the Test Practice Papers in Part 2 of the book.

Revision progress chart

	topic	tick when revised
1	**Number**	✓
1.1	Fractions as parts	✓
1.2	The number line	✓
1.3	Fractions of quantities	✓
1.4	Number pattern	✓
1.5	Decimal number	✓
1.6	Percentage of	✓
1.7	Long multiplication	✓
1.8	Long division	✓
1.9	Negative number arithmetic	✓
1.10	Special numbers	✓
1.11	Decimal places	✓
1.12	Significant figures	✓
1.13	Ratios	✓
1.14	Approximation	✓
1.15	As a percentage	✓

2	**Algebra**	
2.1	Using letters	
2.2	Simplification	
2.3	Generalising a number pattern (the nth term)	
2.4	Combining algebraic expressions	
2.5	Substitution	
2.6	Solving equations	
2.7	Simultaneous equations	
2.8	Expansion	
3	**Graphs**	
3.1	Conversion graphs	
3.2	Travel graphs	
3.3	Graphs from linear equations	
3.4	Solving simultaneous equations graphically	
4	**Mensuration**	
4.1	Area of a rectangle	
4.2	Volume of a cuboid	
4.3	Units	
4.4	Area of a triangle	
4.5	Area of a trapezium	
4.6	Circumference of a circle	
4.7	Area of a circle	
4.8	Volume of a cylinder	
4.9	Volume of prisms	
4.10	Density	
4.11	Pythagoras' theorem	
5	**Geometry and construction**	
5.1	Vertically opposite angles	
5.2	Angles on a line	
5.3	Lines of symmetry	
5.4	Rotational symmetry	
5.5	Angles around a point	
5.6	Angles in a triangle	

5.7	Nets of solid shapes	
5.8	Transformations	
5.9	Parallel lines	
5.10	Special triangles	
5.11	Special quadrilaterals	
5.12	Tessellations	
5.13	Congruency	
5.14	Solid 3-dimensional shapes	
5.15	Angles in a polygon	
6	**Probability and statistics**	
6.1	Charts	
6.2	Averages	
6.3	Frequency tables	
6.4	Grouped data	
6.5	Surveys	
6.6	Simple data collection sheet	
6.7	Questionnaires	
6.8	Scatter diagram	
6.9	Lines of best fit	
6.10	Probability	
6.11	Theoretical probability	
6.12	Experimental probability	
6.13	Probability of NOT happening	

1.1 Fractions as parts LEVEL 3

One divided into two equal parts shows two halves ($\frac{1}{2}$).
One divided into **a** __3__ equal parts shows three thirds ($\frac{1}{3}$). ✓
Three-eighths, $\frac{3}{8}$, is illustrated by three equal parts of a whole split into eight parts.

$\frac{1}{2}$	$\frac{1}{2}$

$\frac{1}{3}$	$\frac{1}{3}$	$\frac{1}{3}$

1.2 The number line LEVEL 3

$$-6 \quad -5 \quad -4 \quad -3 \quad -2 \quad -1 \quad 0 \quad 1 \quad 2 \quad 3 \quad 4 \quad 5 \quad 6$$

- The further to the right you go, the greater the numbers are.
- The further to the left you go, the smaller the numbers are.

$<$ means less than, e.g. $3 < 8$ and $-5 < -1$
$>$ means greater than, e.g. $5 > 2$ and $1 > -7$

1.3 Fractions of quantities LEVEL 4

Example ✓

Q Find $\frac{2}{5}$ of 140 grams.

A First find $\frac{1}{5}$ by dividing by 5, then find $\frac{2}{5}$ by **b**  multiplying by 2.
i.e. $140 \div 5 = 28$, then $28 \times 2 = 56$ grams

1.4 Number pattern LEVEL 4

A number pattern can be created in all sorts of ways.
For example, 3, 5, 7, 9, 11, 13, we add on 2 every time
1, 2, 4, 7, **c** __11__ , __16__ , we add on 1, then 2, then 3, etc.

1.5 Decimal number LEVEL 4

Change a fraction to a decimal by dividing the top by the bottom.

Example ✓

Q Change $\frac{5}{8}$ to a decimal number.

A Divide 5 by **d** __8__ to give 0.625.

Answers can be found on page 37

1.6 Percentage of LEVEL 4

To find A% of an amount P, you calculate $(A \times P) \div 100$.

For example, 4% of 70 cm is $(4 \times 70) \div$ **e** $100 = 2.8$ cm.

Some common fractions expressed as a percentage are:

$\frac{1}{2} = 50\%$ $\frac{1}{4} = 25\%$ $\frac{3}{4} = 75\%$ $\frac{1}{10} = 10\%$ $\frac{1}{5} =$ **f** 20 % $\frac{1}{3} = 33\frac{1}{3}\%$

1.7 Long multiplication LEVEL 5

To work out 435×27 you would do

```
       435
  ×     27
      3045        (435 multiplied by 7)
      8700        (435 multiplied by 20)
     11745        (the two g added together)
```

1.8 Long division LEVEL 5

Example

Q How many coaches holding 53 each will be needed to take a school party of 623?

A We have to do the division $623 \div 53$ as follows

```
        11
   53)623
        53
        93
        53
        40
```

The answer is that there will be 11 full coaches and 1 coach with **h** 40 on.
So we need to book 12 coaches.

1.9 Negative number arithmetic LEVEL 5

To **add two negative** numbers you should add the *numbers* and then make it negative.
For example, $-5 + -4$ *or* $-5 - 4 = -9$

To **add a negative and a positive** number you should take the smaller away from the
i bigger number and give it the sign of the *bigger number*.
For example, $-10 + 3 = -(10 - 3) = -7$

$4 + -6$ *or* $4 - 6 = -(6 - 4) = -2$

To **subtract a negative number** you should read the $--$ as a $+$.
For example, $8 - -2 = 8 +$ **j** $2 = 10$

Answers can be found on page 37

8

The rules for **multiplying** and **dividing** with negative numbers are very easy.

- If the signs are the same, the answer is a positive.
- If the signs are different, the answer is a negative.

For example,

$$3 \times 4 = 12 \qquad -2 \times -5 = 10 \qquad 18 \div -6 = -3 \qquad -24 \div -3 = 8$$

1.10 Special numbers LEVEL 5

Square numbers are whole numbers multiplied by themselves.
For example, 1 , 4 , 9 , 16 , 25 , k 36 , 49

Factors of A are whole numbers that will divide exactly into A.
For example, the factors of 12 are 1 , 2 , 3 , 4 , l 6 and 12.

Prime numbers are whole numbers that have exactly two factors only.
For example, 2 , 3 , 5 , 7 , 11 , 13 , m 17 , 19

Multiples of A are whole numbers that have been multiplied by A.
For example, some multiples of 5 are 5 , 10 , 15 , n 20 , 25

1.11 Decimal places LEVEL 6

When a number is written in decimal form, the digits on the right-hand side of the decimal point are called the p decimal places

For example, 74.6 is written to 1 decimal place (d.p.), and 0.125 is written to 3 d.p.

Rules to **round** a decimal number off to a particular number of places are:

- Count down the decimal places from the point and look at the first digit you are going to remove.
- If this digit is less than 5 then just remove the unwanted places.
- If this digit is 5 or q more , then add 1 onto the last decimal place digit.

For example, 3.642 will round off to 3.64 to 2 decimal places.

0.475 will round off to 0.5 to 1 decimal place.

19.153 will round off to r 19.2 to 1 decimal place.

1.12 Significant figures LEVEL 6

We often use **significant figures** when we want to approximate a number with quite a few digits in it. The number of significant figures that a number is written to is the number of 'real' digits together in a number before any noughts.

For example, look at this table of various numbers of significant figures (s.f.)

1 s.f.	7	40	300	80000	0.00004	0.002
2 s.f.	84	9.3	0.47	21000	390	0.0053

Answers can be found on page 37

Rules to **round** a number off to a particular number of significant figures are very similar to the rules for decimal places.

- From the left, count down the number of digits to be included within the given significant figure and look at the very next digit.
- If this is less than **S** ⟨5⟩, then leave the digits on the left the same.
- If this digit is not less than 5, then add 1 to the digits on the left. ✓
- Put in enough noughts to keep the number the right size.

For example, rounding to 2 s.f., 0.475 will round off to 0.48 and 475 will round off to 480.

1.13 Ratios LEVEL 6

To divide any amount into a given ratio, you simply multiply the amount by the fraction found from the ratio.

Example

Q Divide 48 marbles between Joy and Thomas in the ratio of 5 : 3.

A We **t** ⟨add⟩ the numbers in the ratio to get 8, then use each number to create the fractions $\frac{5}{8}$ and $\frac{3}{8}$. So we see that Joy receives $\frac{5}{8}$ and Thomas receives $\frac{3}{8}$, that is Joy receives $48 \times \frac{5}{8} = 30$ and Thomas receives $48 \times \frac{3}{8} = 18$

1.14 Approximation LEVEL 7

To **approximate** the answer to the problem 37.3×8.73 and to many other similar situations we simply **U** ⟨round⟩ each number off to 1 significant figure, and then work it out. So, the approximation will be

$$37.3 \times 8.73 \approx 40 \times 9 = 360$$

A quick approximation is always a good help in any calculation since it often stops you writing down a silly answer.

1.15 As a percentage LEVEL 7

To find one quantity as a percentage of another, put them together as a fraction of each other and then convert that **V** ⟨fraction⟩ to a percentage by multiplying by 100.

Example

Q Express 6 kg as a percentage of 75 kg.

A First set up the fraction $\frac{6}{75}$ and multiply by 100. This becomes

$$(6 \div 75) \times 100 = \boxed{W} \; ⟨8⟩ \; \%$$

Answers can be found on page 37

Algebra

2.1 Using letters LEVEL 5

In algebra we use **a** _____ instead of numbers.

For example, one more than x is written as $x + 1$

three less than $4y$ is $4y - 3$

two more than N is written as **b** $N + 2$

five less than $2x$ is written as **c** $2x - 5$

2.2 Simplification LEVEL 5

To **simplify** an expression is to combine all those terms that can be combined. Remember, we can only add (or subtract) terms of the same type, i.e. like terms.

For example,

$$2(3 + t) + 4(3 + 5t) = 6 + 2t + 12 + 20t$$
$$= 18 + \text{ } \textbf{d} \text{ } 22t$$

2.3 Generalising a number pattern (the _n_th term) LEVEL 5

If the pattern is built up by simply adding on the same number each time, then you can use the following technique.

- To generalise 2, 7, 12, 17, 22 (here we are adding **e** 5 on each time) the nth term is given by $2 + 5(n - 1) = 5n - 3$.
- We use the 2 because the pattern started with a **f** 2 .
- We use 5 because we add **g** 5 on each time.

Another common pattern to use is the square numbers.

For example, in the pattern 1, 4, 9, 16, 25, the nth term is n^2.

2.4 Combining algebraic expressions LEVEL 6

We can only add or subtract terms or expressions of the same type.

For example,

$$t + t = 2t \qquad 2x + 5x = 7x \qquad x^2 + 8x^2 = 9x^2$$
$$6p - 2p = 4p \qquad 3w - w = 2w \qquad 8y^2 - 3y^2 = 5y^2$$

When we multiply expressions, we remove the $\times$ sign and we _add_ the powers.

For example,

$$y \times y = y^2 \qquad t \times t \times t = t^3 \qquad p \times p \times p \times p = p^4$$
$$x^2 \times x^3 = x^5 \qquad p^4 \times p^3 = p^7$$

Note that $t = t^1$, $p = p^1$, etc. and $w^0 = 1$, $m^0 = 1$, etc.

Answers can be found on page 37

2.5 Substitution LEVEL 6

The value of an expression such as $4t + 3$ will **h**_____ with the different values of t substituted into it.

For example, when $t = 2$ the expression $4t + 3$ will be

$(4 \times 2) + 3 =$ **i**_____

2.6 Solving equations LEVEL 6

Linear equations

Example

Q Solve $4x + 5 = 15$

A We can move the 5 to give $4x = 15 - 5 = 10$

We can now **j**_____ to give $x = 10 \div 4$

So the solution is $x =$ **k**_____

Trial and improvement

Example

Q Find a solution to the equation $x^3 + x = 50$ giving your solution to 1 decimal place.

A We must first find the two whole numbers that x lies between. We do this by **l**_____ guessing.

Try $x = 3$. This gives $27 + 3 = 30$ Too low, so the next trial needs to be **m**_____

Try $x = 4$. This gives $64 + 4 = 68$ Too high, but we now know that the solution is between 3 and 4

We must now try halfway between 3 and 4, which is 3.5.

Try 3.5. This gives $42.875 + 3.5 = 46.375$ Too small but we can see that we are very close so we can improve the trial by trying 3.6

Try 3.6. This gives $46.656 + 3.6 = 50.256$ Too high

We now know the solution is **n**_____ 3.5 and 3.6, but which is closer?

To find which is closer we shouldn't just look at the numbers we have because the differences do not go up uniformly. We should try halfway between again and go from there. Halfway between 3.5 and 3.6 is 3.55.

Try 3.55, this gives $44.738875 + 3.55 = 48.288875$ Too low.

So the solution is nearest to the higher which is 3.6 (to 1 d.p.)

Answers can be found on page 37

2.7 Simultaneous equations LEVEL 7

Here we try to add or subtract the equations in order to *eliminate* one of the variables.

Example

Q Solve $3x + y = 11$
$2x + y = 9$

A Since both equations have a y term the same we can subtract one equation from the other to give $x = 2$.

We now substitute $x = 2$ into one of the equations (usually the one with smallest numbers involved). So substitute into $2x + y = 9$ to give

$$4 + y = 9$$

which gives $y = 9 - 4$

$$y = \boxed{p}\underline{\hspace{3cm}}$$

We test out our solution in the other of the original equations. Substitute $x = 2$ and $y = 5$ into $3x + y$ to give $6 + 5 = 11$, which is correct, so we can confidently say that our solution is $x = 2$ and $y = 5$.

2.8 Expansion LEVEL 7

To **expand** a bracket situation, you have to multiply each term inside the
$\boxed{q}\underline{\hspace{4cm}}$ by the term on the outside of the bracket.

Some examples of expansion are

$$2(4t + 5) = 8t + 10$$
$$4y(y - 3) = 4y^2 - 12y$$

Answers can be found on page 37

13

topic

3

Graphs

3.1 Conversion graphs LEVEL 4

A conversion graph is a graph used to convert from one type of unit to another.
For example, the graph here illustrates the charges made for electricity in 1997.

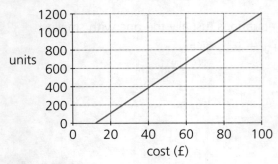

We can see from the graph that:

- If a customer uses 200 units of electricity he will be charged about £ **a** _____.
- If you received a bill for £75 then you will have used around **b** _____ units.

3.2 Travel graphs LEVEL 5

Travel graphs give information about how something has travelled.
From a travel graph you can find information by reading the graph in the same way as in conversion graphs.
You often need to find the average speed from a travel graph by using the simple connection:

$$\text{average speed} = \frac{\text{total distance travelled}}{\text{total time}}$$

Example
The travel graph here represents a coach journey from Birmingham to Bude, a distance of 220 miles.

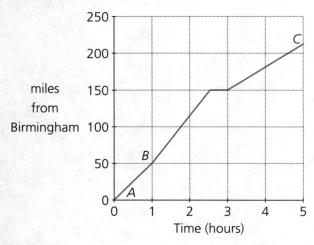

Answers can be found on page 37

We can read from the graph that:

- After 1 hour the coach was **c**_____ miles away from Birmingham.
- After **d**_____ hours the car was 150 miles away from Birmingham.
- The car stopped on the way for **e**_____ an hour.
- It took **f**_____ hours for the complete journey.

We can work out the average speeds as:

- *A* to *B* represents 50 miles in 1 hour which is **g**_____ mph.
- *A* to *C* represents the complete journey of 220 miles in 5 hours. Divide 220 by 5 to give the whole journey's **h**_____ of 44 mph.

3.3 Graphs from linear equations LEVEL 6

These graphs will always give a straight line. You only need three points to be sure of your line.

Example

Q Draw the graph of $y = 3x - 1$.

A Choose different values of *x*. To see what the corresponding value of *y* is you substitute the value for *x* that you have chosen into $y = 3x - 1$, for example:

x	0	2	4
y	−1	5	11

Now plot these points on a grid and join up the points to see the straight line.

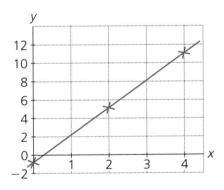

Every linear equation can be written in the form of $y = mx + c$.

If this is then graphed you will always find that $m = $ the **i**_____ of the line and $c = $ the place where the line cuts the **j**_____

This means that if we know the gradient, *m*, of a line is, say 2, and we know the intercept, *c*, of the line with the *y*-axis is, say 5, then we can write down the **k**_____ of the line as $y = 2x + 5$.

Answers can be found on page 37

Note that when you see the equation written in the form $ax + by = c$, this type of equation can be drawn very easily without much working at all.

The following is known as the **cover and draw** method.

Example

Q Draw the graph of the equation $3x + 2y = 12$.

A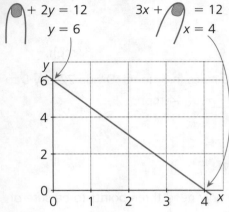

3.4 Solving simultaneous equations graphically LEVEL 6

Example

Q By drawing the graphs find the solution of the simultaneous equations

    a $4x + 3y = 12$ **b** $y = 2x - 1$

A **a** The first graph is drawn using the cover and draw method. It crosses the x-axis at (3, 0) and the y-axis at (0, 4).

    b This graph can be drawn by finding some points say $(0, -1)$, (1, 1) and (3, 5).

Putting this altogether gives the graphs shown here.

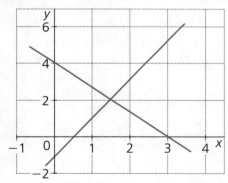

Hence we can see that the point where the graphs **I**_____ is (1.5, 2).

The solution to the simultaneous equations is $x = 1.5$, $y = 2$.

Answers can be found on page 37

4 Mensuration

4.1 Area of a rectangle LEVEL 3

The area of a rectangle is found by multiplying the **a**_____ by the **b**_____ .

4.2 Volume of a cuboid LEVEL 5

The volume of a cuboid is given by **length × breadth × height**.

Example

Q Find the volume of the cuboid shown.

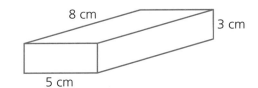

8 cm   3 cm   5 cm

A The volume = length × breadth × height
$$= 8\,\text{cm} \times 5\,\text{cm} \times 3\,\text{cm}$$
$$= \boxed{\text{c}}_____ \text{cm}^3$$

Note that sometimes the height will be referred to as depth.

4.3 Units LEVEL 5

You do need to be familiar with the metric units such as:

10 mm = 1 cm	100 cm = 1 m	1000 m = 1 km
1000 g = 1 kg	1000 kg = 1 tonne	1000 cm³ = 1 litre

You also need to know the approximate equivalences of imperial measures to metric:

1 inch = 2.5 **d**_____   2.2 pounds = 1 **e**_____   4.5 litres = **f**_____

4.4 Area of triangle LEVEL 6

The area of a triangle is calculated as **half of the base length × the g**_____

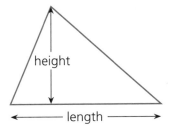

height

length

Answers can be found on page 37

Example

Q Find the area of this triangle.

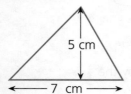

5 cm

7 cm

A The area $= \frac{1}{2} \times 7\,cm \times 5\,cm = $ **h**_____ cm²

4.5 Area of trapezium LEVEL 6

To find the area of a trapezium, calculate the average length of the parallel sides and multiply this by the vertical difference between them. In other words

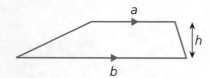

i.e. area $= \dfrac{h(a+b)}{2}$

Example

Q Find the area of the trapezium *ABCD*.

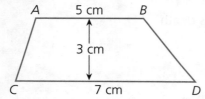

A The area is given by

$3 \times \dfrac{(5+7)}{2}$ which equals **i**_____ cm²

4.6 Circumference of a circle LEVEL 6

circumference = π × diameter

Do not forget that the value for π is best found by pressing its button on your calculator, but if you have not got access to that button then 3.14 is a good approximation to use.

Example 1

Q Find the circumference of a circle with a diameter of 8 cm.

A Use the formula $C = \pi D = \pi \times 8 = $ **j**_____ cm (1 d.p.)

Answers can be found on page 37

Example 2

Q Find the circumference of a circle with a radius of 6 cm.

A First you need to double the radius to get the diameter, 12 cm.
   Then you can use $C = \pi D = \pi \times 12 = $ **k**_____ cm (1 d.p.)

4.7 Area of a circle LEVEL 6

The area of a circle is given by the rule

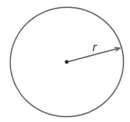

area = πr^2

Be careful! This formula uses radius, but if the information you are given is the diameter then you will need to halve the diameter to get your radius.

Example – with the radius given

Q Find the area of a circle with a radius of 3 cm.

A area $= \pi r^2 = \pi \times 3^2 = \pi \times 9$ (use π on the calculator)
   $= $ **l**_____ cm^2 (rounded to 1 d.p.)

Example – with the diameter given

Q Find the area of a circle with a diameter of 10 cm.

A First halve the diameter to get a radius of 5 cm. Then use

   area $= \pi r^2 = \pi \times 5^2 = \pi \times 25 = $ **m**_____ cm^2 (rounded to 1 d.p.)

4.8 Volume of a cylinder LEVEL 7

The **volume** of a cylinder is found by multiplying the area of the circular end by the length of the cylinder. That is

   volume = $\pi r^2 h$ (where r = radius and h = height or length)

Example

Q What is the volume of a cylinder with radius 5 cm and height 9 cm?

A volume = base area × height
   $= \pi r^2 \times h$
   $= \pi \times 5^2 \times 9 = $ **n**_____ cm^3 (rounded)

Answers can be found on page 37

19

4.9 Volume of prisms LEVEL 7

A prism is a solid shape that has the same cross-section running all the way through it, as shown in the diagram.

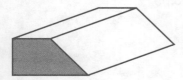

The volume of a prism is found by **p**_____ the area of the regular cross-section by its length (or height if stood on end). That is

volume of prism = area of cross-section × length

4.10 Density LEVEL 7

Density is the amount of weight per unit of volume, usually given in grams per cubic centimetre, i.e. g/cm^3.

Remember that weight is commonly used in mathematics examination questions whereas in science they always refer to it as mass. The connection between the three is

$$density = \frac{weight}{volume}$$

This connection is often remembered with a triangle. This reminds you that

weight = density × volume

density = weight ÷ volume

q_____ = weight ÷ density

Example

Q What is the weight of a rock that is $29\,cm^3$ and has a density of $1.7\,g/cm^3$?

A weight = 29 × 1.7 = **r**_____ g

4.11 Pythagoras' theorem LEVEL 7

'In any right angled triangle the sum of the squares of the lengths of the two short sides is equal to the square of the **s**_____*.'*

Example

Q Find the length of the hypotenuse x in the diagram.

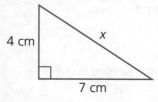

A $x^2 = 7^2 + 4^2 = 49 + 16 = 65$

$x = \sqrt{65} =$ **t**_____ cm (1 d.p.)

Answers can be found on page 37

Geometry and construction

5.1 Vertically opposite angles LEVEL 3

The angles marked vertically opposite to each other are equal.

5.2 Angles on a line LEVEL 3

The angles on a straight line add up to 180°, i.e. in the diagrams here $a + b = 180°$ and $x + y + z = 180°$.

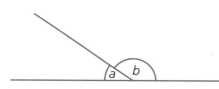

5.3 Lines of symmetry LEVEL 3

A way to recognise a **line of symmetry** is to see if the shape can be folded on the line of symmetry so that both halves fall exactly on top of each other as shown.

line of symmetry   folded

5.4 Rotational symmetry LEVEL 4

A flat shape has **rotational symmetry** if it can be rotated about a point in such a way that it looks just the same in the new position.

Look at the shapes in the diagram here. They each have **a** _____ as you can rotate them about the dot so that they look the same in another position.

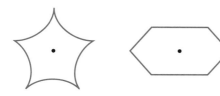

This dot is called the **point of symmetry**.

Answers can be found on page 37

21

Order of rotational symmetry

The **order** of rotational symmetry of any shape is given by the number of different positions in which the shape looks the same when it is rotated about its point of

b_____. (Like the centre of rotation in transformation geometry.)

Examples

A parallelogram has rotational symmetry of order 2.

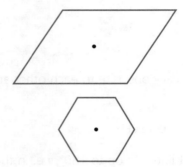

A regular hexagon has rotational symmetry of order 6.

Note that *every* shape has an **order** of symmetry but a shape only has **rotational symmetry** if its order is 2 or higher.

For example, this 'A' shape has rotational symmetry of order 1. However, we still say it has *no* rotational symmetry.

5.5 Angles around a point LEVEL 4

The sum of the angles around a point is 360°, i.e. $a + b + c + d = 360°$

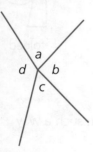

5.6 Angles in a triangle LEVEL 4

The three angles in a triangle all add up to 180°.

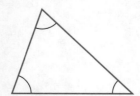

Answers can be found on page 37

5.7 Nets of solid shapes LEVEL 4

A net of a solid shape is the shape drawn out onto a piece of paper or card in such a way that if you cut round the whole shape you could fold it up into the solid shape.

For example, a net of a cuboid is shown here

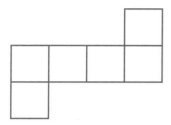

This could be folded up into a **C**_____ .

5.8 Transformations LEVELS 4-5

The particular change of position of shapes you need to be familiar with are:
*   Translation – LEVEL 4
*   Reflection – LEVEL 4
*   Rotation – LEVEL 5
*   Enlargement – LEVEL 5

All of these changes, except enlargement, keep a shape congruent but change position.

Translation

A **translation** is a movement of a shape from one place to another without reflecting it or rotating it.

We describe these changes of position using column vectors which are a description of how to move from one point to another using horizontal shift and vertical shift.

For example, the vector describing the translation from A to B in the diagram is $\begin{pmatrix} 3 \\ 1 \end{pmatrix}$.

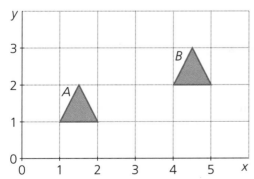

*   The top number describes the horizontal movement, −ve means move left.
*   The bottom number describes the vertical movement, −ve means move down.

Answers can be found on page 37

Reflection

A **reflection** is what you see when you look in a 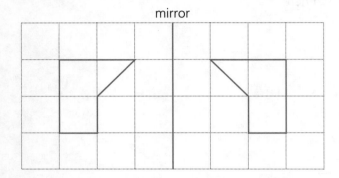 d _____ at right angles to it. An example is shown here. Note that the reflection of each point is perpendicular to the mirror line.

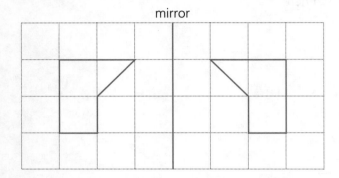

If you 'fold' over the mirror line then any point and its reflection should be on top of each other.

Rotations

A **rotation** of a shape is that shape turned as a whole around some particular point called **centre of rotation**.

An example is shown here.

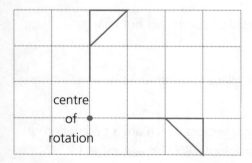

Notice:

- The angle given has direction usually given by e _____ or anticlockwise.
- The centre of rotation is always specified, here it is by the dot.
- The most common exam rotations are 90° and 180° around the origin.

Enlargement

An **enlargement** always has a **centre of enlargement**, and a **scale factor**. Every length of the enlargement will be:

original length × scale factor

The distance of each image point on the enlargement from the centre of enlargement will be:

the distance from the original point to the centre of enlargement × scale factor

Answers can be found on page 37

For example, the enlargement of scale factor 2 of triangle *ABC* is:

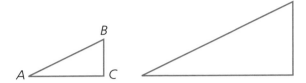

centre of
enlargement

There are two distinct ways to find an enlargement, the **ray method** and the
co-ordinate method.

Ray method
This is the way to find the enlargement if the diagram is not on a grid.
For example, an enlargement of scale factor 2 of triangle *ABC* from the centre of
enlargement is:

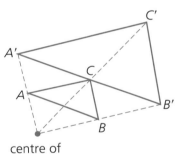

centre of
enlargement

Co-ordinate method
This is perhaps the easiest way to enlarge a shape.
For example, an enlargement of scale factor 2
of triangle *ABC* from the centre of enlargement
is shown here.

Count the squares from the centre of
enlargement to each point and then
simply double this.
So, the movement from the
centre of enlargement to
point *B* is (1 along and 2 up),
this becomes (2 along and 4 up) to *B'*.

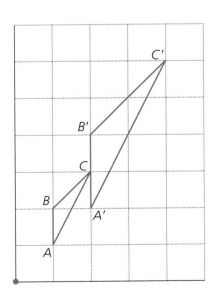

Answers can be found on page 37

5.9 Parallel lines LEVEL 5

The diagram shows two parallel lines
(the arrows indicate that they are parallel).
The line cutting through the parallel lines is called
a **transversal**. You can see in the diagram that this
creates equal angles.
The correct name for these equal angles is **alternate
angles** but they are often called **Z angles** since that
is what they look like.

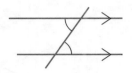

Parallel lines also create **allied angles**
as shown in the diagram here, where
the two 'allied' angles shown will add up to 180°.

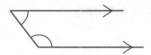

5.10 Special triangles LEVEL 5

Equilateral triangle

An equilateral triangle has all its sides
the same **f**_____ and each of its
interior angles is 60°.

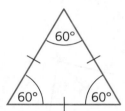

Isosceles triangle

An isosceles triangle has two of its sides
the same length and two of its
g_____ are equal.

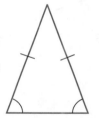

5.11 Special quadrilaterals LEVEL 5

Trapezium

- A trapezium has one pair of opposite
  sides parallel. The angles at the same end
  of the parallel lines add up to 180°.

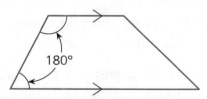

Parallelogram

- A parallelogram has both opposite sides **h**_____ .
- The opposite sides are equal in length.
- The diagonals of a quadrilateral bisect each other.
- The **i**_____ angles of a parallelogram
  are equal to each other,
  i.e. $\angle A = \angle C$ and $\angle B = \angle D$

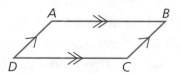

Answers can be found on page 37

Rhombus

- A rhombus is a parallelogram with all its sides the same length.
- The 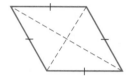 of a rhombus bisect each other at right angles.
- The diagonals of a rhombus bisect the angles.

Kite

- A kite is a quadrilateral with two pairs of equal adjacent sides.
- The longer diagonal bisects the other diagonal at right angles.
- The angles between the different lengths are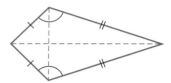

5.12 Tessellations LEVEL 5

Tessellations are another form of symmetry within plane flat surfaces.
A tessellation is a regular pattern made with just 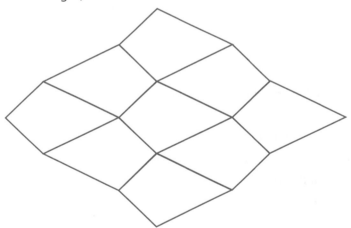 shape in such a way that that shape would fill the whole of a huge flat surface and leave no gaps (except perhaps at the edges).

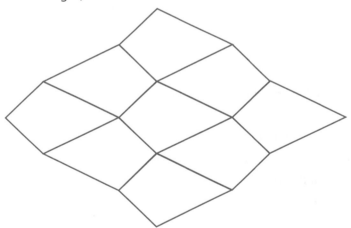

5.13 Congruency LEVEL 6

Shapes that are identical to each other in size and angles are said to be congruent to each other. For example, these triangles are all congruent.

Notice that the triangles can be in a different orientation (turned around).

Answers can be found on page 37

5.14 Solid 3-dimensional shapes LEVEL 6

A good way to draw a solid shape
is by using an isometric grid.

Notice that you *must* have the isometric
paper the right way up as shown.

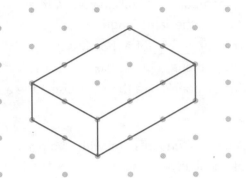

5.15 Angles in a polygon LEVEL 7

Interior angles

For an *N*-sided polygon the interior angles
will add up to $180° \times (N - 2)$.

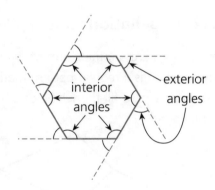

Regular polygons

Regular polygons are those that have every interior angle equal and each side the same
length.

- The exterior angle and the interior angle add up to 180°.
- The exterior angle of a regular *N*-sided polygon is equal to $360° \div N$.
- The interior angle of a regular *N*-sided polygon is equal to 180° − exterior angle

$$= 180° - (360° \div N)$$

Example 1

Q What is the angle sum of a regular 8-sided polygon?

A Angle sum $= 180° \times (8 - 2) =$ **m** _____ °

Example 2

Q What are the sizes of the exterior and the interior angles of a regular
polygon with 15 sides?

A exterior angle $= 360° \div$ **n** _____ $=$ **p** _____ °

interior angle $= 180° -$ **q** _____ $=$ **r** _____ °

Answers can be found on page 37

Probability and statistics

6.1 Charts LEVEL 4

Statistical information is often presented in chart form such as pictograms, bar charts or pie charts.

Bar charts

A bar chart is a very simple chart where you show the frequency of various items of data.

Pie charts

Pie charts look like a pie which has been cut into slices to show the proportion of the different ingredients of the pie.

Example

Q Draw a pie chart to illustrate the following information.

Transport	Bus	Car	Bike	Walk	Train
Frequency	459	123	53	95	20

A We need to find the fraction of 360° that each type of transport represents. This is usually done in a table such as the one below (note we round off the angles).

Transport	Frequency	Calculation	Angle
bus	459	$\frac{459}{750} \times 360$	$\approx 220°$
car	123	$\frac{123}{750} \times 360$	$\approx 59°$
bike	53	$\frac{53}{750} \times 360$	$\approx 25°$
walk	95	$\frac{95}{750} \times 360$	$\approx 46°$
train	20	$\frac{20}{750} \times 360$	$\approx 10°$
total	**750**		**360°**

Note that:

- You use the total 750 to calculate each fraction.
- You round off each angle to the nearest degree.
- You check that all the angles do add up to 360°.

Answers can be found on page 37

The pie chart can now be drawn. Remember it is always good practice to draw the smallest angle first, then the next smallest and so on until the last angle will automatically be the a _____ . This is so that the errors that inevitably add up at the last angle have the least effect on the proportion of the angle to show.

The pie chart should look like the one shown here.

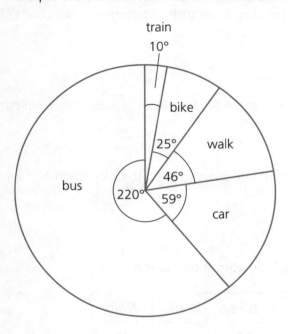

train
10°
bike
25°
walk
46°
bus
220°
59°
car

6.2 **Averages** LEVEL 4

- The **mode** is the item of data that occurs the b _____ .

- The **median** is the item in the c _____ once all the data have been put in size order.

- The **mean** is the result found by d _____ all the data together and dividing the total by how many items of data you started off with.

- The **range** is the difference between the highest and the e _____ number in the data.

Example

Q Find the mode, median, mean and range from 1, 1, 1, 2, 3, 5, 5, 9, 12.

A The **mode** is 1 since this occurs three times (more than any other).

The **median** is 3 since this item is the f _____ item of data.

The **mean** is 4.3 since when the items are added and then g _____ by the number of items you get 39 ÷ 9 which is 4.3 (to 1 d.p.).

The **range** is 11 since the largest number, 12, minus the smallest number, 1 is 11.

Answers can be found on page 37

6.3 Frequency tables LEVEL 5

When a lot of information has been gathered it is convenient to put it together in a frequency table. From this you can then find what the various **h**_____ are.

For example, a survey was done on the number of people sat at a table in a fast food restaurant. The results are summarised in the frequency table below.

Number of people	0	1	2	3	4	5
Frequency	2	3	10	23	25	4

a The **modal** number of people sat at a table is easy to see: it is the number with the largest frequency of 25. Hence the **i**_____ number sat at a table was 4.

b The **median** number of people at the tables is found by working out where the middle is. We can add up the frequency to get 67 people that were surveyed. This gives the middle position as $(67 + 1) \div 2$ which is 34. We now need to count the frequencies along the table until we find which group the 34th person is in. This is found in the group with 3 at a table. So the **j**_____ number sat at a table is 3.

c The **mean** number of people at a table is to be found by adding all the people together and **k**_____ by the number of tables. The calculation for this is shown in the following table.

Number at the table	Frequency	People at the tables
0	2	$0 \times 2 = 0$
1	3	$1 \times 3 = 3$
2	10	$2 \times 10 = 20$
3	23	$3 \times 23 = 69$
4	25	$4 \times 25 = 100$
5	4	$5 \times 4 = 20$
total	**67**	**212**

The mean is then found by $212 \div 67 = 3.1641791$
Hence the mean number of people at a table is 3.2 (to 1 d.p.)

6.4 Grouped data LEVEL 7

Sometimes the information we are given is grouped together, as in the table below which shows the age ranges of people on a coach party.

Age (years)	0–5	6–10	11–17	18–30	31–60
No. of people	6	4	8	23	15

Answers can be found on page 37

The **modal** group is the one with the largest frequency, which is the 18–30 group.

The median will be in the middle of a group, and the way we find it is to draw a particular type of graph called a **cumulative curve**.

The mean can only be estimated since we do not have all the information. To estimate the mean we simply estimate each person in each group to have the 'midway' amount and we build up a table as below.

We find the midway value by adding the two end values together and then dividing by 2. We could round this off to the nearest whole number if we wished since it is only an estimate, but it is usual not to do this rounding off until the very last moment.

Age	Frequency (f)	Midway (m)	f × m	Total
0–5	6	2.5	6 × 2.5	15
6–10	4	8	4 × 8	32
11–17	8	14	8 × 14	112
18–30	23	24	23 × 24	552
31–60	15	45.5	15 × 45.5	682.5
total	56			1393.5

The estimated ▮▮▮▮▮▮ will be 1393.5 ÷ 56 = 24.9 (rounded off).

You will come across a few different ways of labelling the columns (groups) in a grouped frequency table. For example, the groups in the above table might have been labelled

Age (p) (years)	$0 \leqslant p \leqslant 5$	$6 < p \leqslant 10$	$10 < p \leqslant 17$	$17 < p \leqslant 30$	$30 < p < 60$

For group 3 ($10 < p \leqslant 17$) their age is more than 10 years old but less than or equal to 17 years.

You will see different ways of using the inequalities in this type of table. It will make no difference to the middle value as you still use the average of the end-points.

6.5 Surveys LEVEL 4

A survey is an organised way of asking a lot of people a few well constructed questions, or making a lot of observations in an experiment in order to reach a conclusion about something.

Answers can be found on page 37

6.6 Simple data collection sheet LEVEL 4

If you need simply to collect some data in order to carry out some analysis then you want to design a simple data capture sheet.

Example

Q **Which day of the week do you want the form ramble?**

A You can ask a lot of pupils one day and put the results straight onto a data capture sheet like the one below.

	Tally	Total
Sunday	ЖГ |||	
Monday	|||	
Tuesday	||	
Wednesday	ЖГ ||	
Thursday	||	
Friday	ЖГ ЖГ ||	
Saturday	|||	

Notice how we made a large space for **m**_____ , and note how we gate the tallies to give groups of fives which makes it easier to count up once the survey is complete.

This is a good simple data collection sheet since each person asked can easily be given a tally on the sheet and then we can move on to the next person, since we are only concerned with the one question 'which day do you want to go?' and we have a list of responses that we use on the sheet.

6.7 Questionnaires LEVEL 6

When asking questions on a questionnaire you have to be careful to note the following points:

- Never ask leading questions designed to get a particular response.
- Never ask personal, or irrelevant questions.
- Always keep the questions as simple as possible.
- Always set a question that will get an **n**_____ from whoever is asked.

Answers can be found on page 37

The following types of question are **bad questions** and should not appear on any of your questionnaires:

- *What is your age?*
  This is personal, many will not want to answer.
- *Slaughtering poor defenceless animals to test new drugs is cruel, don't you agree?*
  This is a leading question, designed to get a 'yes'.
- *Do you go by hovercraft when you travel to France?*
  This can only be answered by those people who have been to France.
- *Would you rather have maths every day for a shorter time or would you want to have longer maths lessons and less of them or something else?*
  This is a rather complicated question.

The following types of questions are **good questions** in contrast to the poor ones above.

- *In which age group are you? 0–10, 11–15, 16–20, over 20.*
- *Do you think it is cruel to use animals in order to test new drugs?*
- *If you went to France would you use the hovercraft?*
- *Would you like shorter maths lessons every day?*

6.8 Scatter diagram LEVEL 6

A scatter diagram is a graph that plots quite a few points representing *two* things. A scatter diagram is used to see if there is any connection between one thing and another. This connection is called a **correlation**.

The scatter graphs below represent the three different types of P_____ that can be found.

Example 1

Q **Do older pupils get more pocket money?**
(See graph a.)

A This diagram shows positive (or direct) correlation. It shows that as pupils get older, they get more pocket money.

Answers can be found on page 37

Example 2

Q Is there a connection between age
and the number of hours of
sleep needed? (See graph b.)

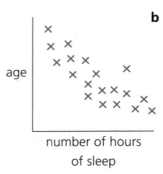

A This diagram shows negative (or indirect) correlation. It shows that the older you are,
the less sleep you need.

Example 3

Q Is there a connection between
temperature and the amount
of bread sold? (See graph c.)

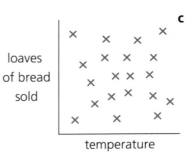

A This diagram shows no correlation. It shows there is no connection between
temperature and amount of bread sold.

6.9 **Lines of best fit** LEVEL 7

If we see there is a correlation between
two things then we can draw a line of best fit.
This is a line that follows the trend of the plotted data.

When you draw this line of best fit you
should be trying to:

- Show the trend.
- Have as many points above the line as below the line.
- Draw the line from one side of the available graph to the other.

But beware:

- This line DOES NOT have to go through all the points.
- This line DOES NOT have to go through the origin.
- This line is NOT drawn from the first to the last point.

This line is usually straight but it could be curved. However, until you get to A-Level
Statistics, all the lines of best fit you will meet should be straight lines.

Answers can be found on page 37

6.10 Probability LEVEL 3

The definition of probability is:

$$P(\text{event}) = \frac{\text{number of ways the event can happen}}{\text{total number of possible outcomes}}$$

This definition always leads to a fraction. If possible the fraction should be cancelled down.

6.11 Theoretical probability LEVEL 5

The theoretical probability is found by considering equally likely events.

Equally likely events are those that all have an equal chance of happening.
For example, equally likely events are like rolling one dice and getting a 1, 2, 3, 4, 5 or 6.
Whereas, events that are *not* equally likely are like rolling two dice and getting the totals 2, 3, 4, 5, 6, 7, etc. Can you see why?

The theoretical probability of an event is found by the fraction:

$$\text{theoretical probability} = \frac{\text{the number of ways the event can happen}}{\text{total number of different equally likely events that can occur}}$$

Two examples are

Probability of rolling a dice and getting a 4 $= \frac{1}{6}$
Probability of tossing a coin and getting a tail $=$ **q** _____

6.12 Experimental probability LEVEL 6

This can be found by performing an experiment many times or making an observation many times, and keeping an accurate record of the result.
The experimental probability of a particular event happening can then be worked out as:

$$\text{experimental probability} = \frac{\text{number of times the event has happened}}{\text{total number of observations}}$$

For example, a normal dice was rolled 200 times; the number 5 was actually rolled a total of 37 times. This gives an experimental probability of

$$\frac{37}{200} = 0.185$$

6.13 Probability of NOT happening LEVEL 6

The probability of an event *not* happening is found by subtracting the probability of it happening from 1.

For example, the probability of snow in March is 0.15.
The probability of *no* snow in March will be

$$1 - 0.15 = \boxed{\textbf{r}} _____$$

Answers can be found on page 37

Test A

Paper 1 With a calculator (Time: 1 hour)

Tips before you start:

- You *can* use your calculator in this paper, so do use it where you need to.

- If the question says 'explain', make sure you write your explanation in clear English.

- Read each question carefully. Make sure you answer the question you have been asked and not your own.

- Remember that you can earn marks for a wrong answer, but to do so you need to have shown the method you used to find your answer.

- If you find your mind goes blank on a particular question, then leave it, go on to the next question and come back to this question later.

- Answer every question on the paper as well as you can.

- Use your full time, check over your answers to find the careless mistakes that we all make.

Q1 Draw the lines of symmetry in each of the diagrams below.

a
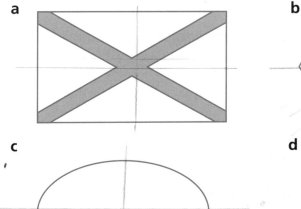

b
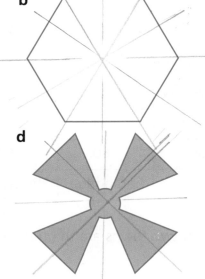

c

d

4

Q1

Answers can be found on page 82

39

Q2 The pictogram shows the number of animals in a zoo.
Each animal in the pictogram stands for 4 actual animals in the zoo.

ANIMALS IN THE ZOO

Chimps	🐒 🐒 🐒
Penguins	🐧 🐧 🐧 🐧 ▯
Lions	🦁 🦁 🦁
Giraffes	▯ ▯

a How many lions are there in the zoo?

. . . . 12 . . . .

b How many chimps are there in the zoo?

. . . . 16 . . . .

c Percy thought there were 18 penguins in the zoo? Explain why
Percy is wrong.

. . . . . . 17 . . . . because the last penguin is a ¼ and
. . . . . . not a ½. . . . .

d Six giraffes are brought into the zoo. Show these on the pictogram.

4

Q2

Q3 This table shows the distances by road between some towns, in miles.

Cambridge			
Shrewsbury	140		
Sheffield	123	114	
London	60	163	168
	Cambridge	Shrewsbury	Sheffield	London

a Which two towns are the furthest distance from each other?

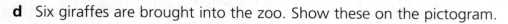

. . . . Sheffield + London . . . .

Answers can be found on page 82

b Geoff drove from Shrewsbury to Cambridge. What distance was this?

. . . . 140 . . . .

c Then Geoff drove from Cambridge to London.
How far did Geoff drive altogether?

. . . . 60 . . . .

. . . 200 . . . .

3
Q3

Q4 Fill in the missing numbers so that the answer is always 34.

a 20 + 14 . . . . = 34

b 143 − 109 . . . . = 34

c 340 ÷ 10 . . . . . = 34

d $\frac{1}{3}$ of 102 . . . . = 34

e 50% of 68 . . . . . = 34

5
Q4

Level 4

Q5 Each side of this hexagon tile is 1 cm long.

a The shaded shape is made from 5 hexagon tiles.

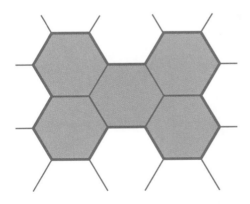

What is the perimeter of this shaded shape?

. . . . 18cm . . . .

Answers can be found on page 82

b Draw a shape made with 5 tiles which has a smaller perimeter.
Label it B.

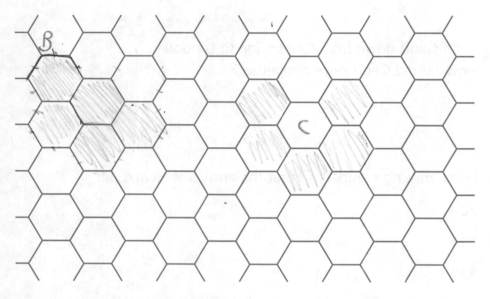

c Draw a shape made with 5 tiles which has the largest possible perimeter and label it C.

d Explain what shapes will have the smallest and the longest possible perimeters.

...the tile close have a small perimeter butt...
..spread out ones have a longer perimeter..

....

4

Q5

Q6 **a** Three points on this line are marked with X.

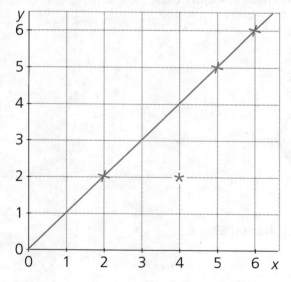

Answers can be found on page 83

42

Their co-ordinates are (2, 2), (5, 5) and (6, 6).
Look at the numbers in the co-ordinates of each point on the line.
What do you notice?

.... The x co-ordinate and the y co-ordinate,
.... are the same.

b The point (?, 15) is on the line. Write down what this co-ordinate is.

.... 15

c The point * is below the line.
Which of the following points are below the line?
(8, 8) (7, 8) (11, 9) or (15, 16)

.... (11, 9)

d The point (A, 20) is a point below the line.
Write down a possible value for A.

.. 21

4
Q6

Q7 **a** Here is a number chain: 3 → 6 → 9 → 12 → 15 →
The rule is: add 3 on each time.
A different number chain is: 3 → 9 → 27 → 81 → 243 →
What could this rule be?

.... ×3

1
Q7a

b Some number chains start like this: 1 → 4 →
Show three different ways to continue this number chain.
For each chain write down the next three numbers and write down
the rule you are using.

i 1 → 4 → 7, 10, 13. add 3

ii 1 → 4 → 16, 64, 254 multiply × 4

iii 1 → 4 → 8, 13, 19

3
Q7b

Answers can be found on page 83

43

Q8 Sid bought a baby snake.

a The scale shows how long the baby snake was when she was bought.

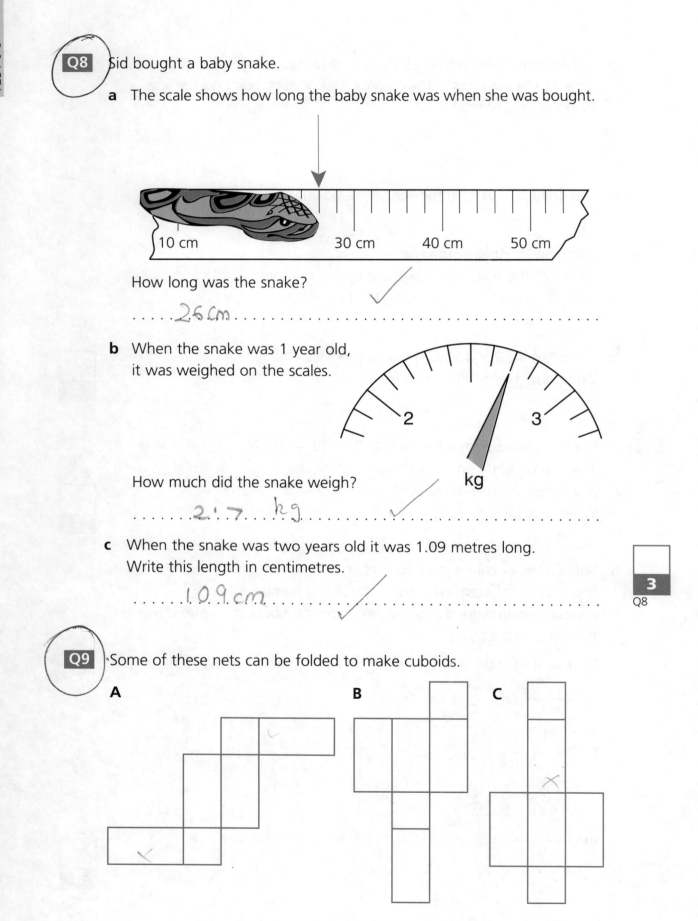

10 cm   30 cm   40 cm   50 cm

How long was the snake?

........26 cm..................

b When the snake was 1 year old, it was weighed on the scales.

2   3

kg

How much did the snake weigh?

.......2·7 kg.......................

c When the snake was two years old it was 1.09 metres long. Write this length in centimetres.

.......109 cm.........................

3
Q8

Q9 Some of these nets can be folded to make cuboids.

A   **B**   **C**

Answers can be found on page 83

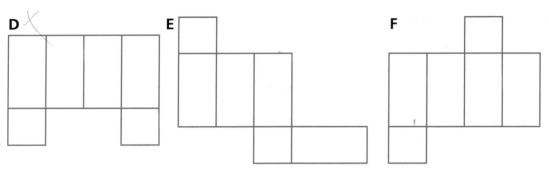

D   E   F

   a   Which of these nets cannot be folded to make cuboids?

         . . . . A c D . . . .

   b   Show clearly on a diagram what is wrong with each of the nets
        that will not make a cuboid.

4

Q9

Q10   I can either catch the Thompson Bus or the Coachline Bus for my
        journey to school each morning.
        This is how long I had to wait for the Thompson Bus last week

         9 min   7 min   9 min   8 min   7 min

        This is how long I had to wait for the Coachline Bus

         17 min   1 min   2 min   16 min   1 min

   a   For each bus, calculate the mean and the range of the times.

       . . . .

       . . . . 40 ÷ 5 = 8 . . . . . . ✓ . . . . 7 – 9 . . . .

       . . . . 37 ÷ 5 = 7·4 . . ✓ . . . . 1 – 17 . . . .

       . . . .

       . . . .

4

Q10a

   b   Use the mean and the range to choose which bus is best to catch.

       . . . .

       . . . .

       . . . .

1

Q10b

Answers can be found on page 83

Q11 Bill has three cards, numbered 3, 5 and 7.

Anne has three cards numbered 6, 8 and 9.

They each select one of their three cards.

They then subtract the smallest number from the largest (in this pair).

a Write down all the possible combinations of their two cards and their differences.

3,6 = 3 ✓ 7,6 = 1 ✓ 9,6 = 3 8,3 = 5

5,8 = 3 7,8 = 1 9,5 = 4 6,5 = 1 ✓

7,9 = 2 8,9 = 1 9,3 = 6 ✓

2
Q11a

b What is the probability that their answer is an odd number?

$\frac{6}{9}$

1
Q11b

c What is the probability that their answer is a number less than 5?

$\frac{7}{9}$

1
Q11c

Level 5

Q12 Bina drew these rectangles using a computer.

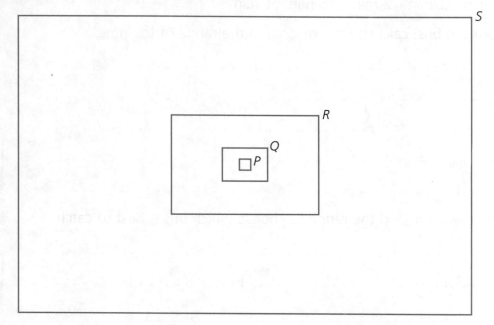

Answers can be found on page 84

46

The rectangle *P* has a width of 1 and a length of 2.
The computer repeats these instructions to draw the other rectangles:

new width = previous width × 3
new length = previous length + new width.

Complete this table:

	Width	Length
rectangle *P*	1	2
rectangle *Q*	3	5
rectangle *R*	9	14
rectangle *S*	27	41

3
Q12

Q13 The perimeter of this shape
is $7t + 2m + 1$.
Write an expression for the
perimeters of each of these shapes.
Write each expression in its simplest form.

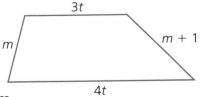

a

b

c

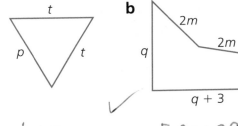

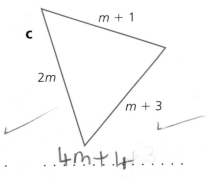

$2t + p$ ...... $5m + 2q + 3$ .. $4m + 4$ ......

3
Q13

Q14 Steve had these 6 sticks.

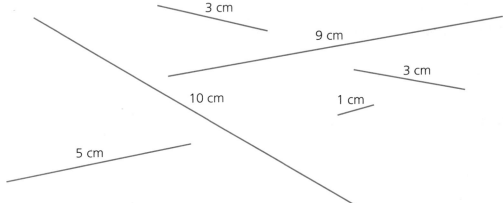

He picked up three sticks and found that he could make a triangle
with them.

Answers can be found on page 84

47

a Which three sticks could Steve have chosen?

...... 3cm. 3cm. 5cm ....

....

....

....

b Choose three sticks that will not make a triangle.

...... 10 cm. 9cm. 1cm ....

c Explain why these three sticks do not form a triangle.

....

....

Q15 The two frequency diagrams below show the hours of sunshine during two different months.

Month A

Month B

a How many days are there in month A?

.... 2 + 4 + 8 + 9 + 7 = 30 ....

b Explain the differences between month A and month B.

.... more days with less sunshine ....

....

....

....

Answers can be found on page 84

Q16 From the numbers in the cloud illustrated
 a Write down which are square numbers.

. . . .

. . . .

 b Write down which are prime numbers.

. . . .

7
4   9
28
25   23   16   11

4
Q16

Q17 Joy was given money for her birthday from her brother, her dad, her uncle and her cousin.
Her brother gave her £ *N*.

 a Her cousin gave her as much as her brother.
  How much did her cousin give her?

. . . .

 b Her uncle gave her three times as much as her brother.
  How much did her uncle give her?

. . . .

 c Dad gave her £10 more than her brother.
  How much did dad give her?

. . . .

 d How much was Joy given altogether from the four people?

. . . .

. . . .

4
Q17

Q18 The same measurement is often given in different units.
On each container below write the correct units.
Choose your units from:

  grams   litres   pints   pounds   kilograms   inches

 a Weight of
  marmalade.

Marmalade
l . . . .
450 . . . . . .

 b Bottle of
  lemonade

lemonade
3 . . . .
5.3 . . . .

4
Q18

Answers can be found on page 84

Paper 2 Without a calculator (Time: 1 hour)

Tips before you start:

- You *cannot* use your calculator in this paper, so be prepared for those questions where you need to make the calculations yourself.

- If the question says 'explain', make sure you write your explanation in clear English.

- Read each question carefully. Make sure you answer the question you have been asked and not your own.

- Remember that you can earn marks for a wrong answer, but to do so you need to have shown the method you used to find your answer.

- If you find your mind goes blank on a particular question, then leave it, go on to the next question and come back to this question later.

- Answer every question on the paper as well as you can.

- Use your full time, check over your answers to find the careless mistakes that we all make.

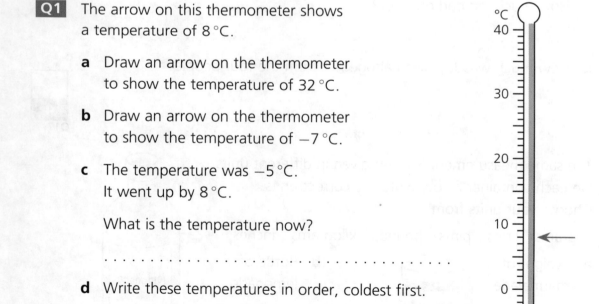

Q1 The arrow on this thermometer shows a temperature of 8 °C.

a Draw an arrow on the thermometer to show the temperature of 32 °C.

b Draw an arrow on the thermometer to show the temperature of −7 °C.

c The temperature was −5 °C. It went up by 8 °C.

What is the temperature now?

. . . .

d Write these temperatures in order, coldest first.

   4 °C   −6 °C   1 °C   15 °C   −3 °C

. . . .

. . . .

4

Q1

Answers can be found on page 85

Q2 **a** Joseph went to the cinema with Helen and paid £6.80 with a £10 note.
How much change should Joseph get?

. . . .

. . . .

. . . .

1

Q2a

b In one month, Joseph took Helen to the cinema 14 times and paid £6.80 each time.
How much did Joseph pay at the cinema altogether?

. . . .

. . . .

. . . .

. . . .

2

Q2b

c A group went to the cinema and paid £30.60 for their tickets.
Each ticket cost £3.40. How many were in the group?

. . . .

. . . .

. . . .

2

Q2c

Q3 Dean and Kirsty each have 24 biscuits.

a Dean eats one-third of his biscuits. How many biscuits has he eaten?

. . . .

1

Q3a

b Kirsty eats 6 of her 24 biscuits. What fraction of her biscuits does she eat?

. . . .

. . . .

1

Q3b

c How many biscuits are left altogether?

. . . .

. . . .

2

Q3c

Answers can be found on page 85

Q4 **a** Donna puts 4 white beads and 1 blue bead into a bag.
She takes a bead out of the bag without looking.
Which colour bead is she more likely to get, and why?

. . . .

. . . .

b Robert puts 7 white beads and 1 blue bead into a bag.
Janet is going to take a bead without looking and she wants to get a
white bead. Should she take a bead from Donna's or Robert's bag?
Explain why.

. . . .

. . . .

. . . .

c The arrow shows the
probability that Donna
gets a blue bead
from her bag.

Donna's
bag

0   1

Put an arrow on the line to show the probability that Robert gets a
blue bead from his bag. Label the arrow R.

d Leigh puts two blue beads and 1 white bead in a bag.
What is the chance that Leigh gets a white bead when he takes a
bead from his bag?

. . . .

. . . .

e Put an arrow on the line above to show the probability that Leigh
gets a white bead from his bag. Label the arrow L.

5
Q4

Level 4

Q5 State the order of rotational symmetry for each of the following shapes.

a

. . . .

b

. . . .

Answers can be found on page 85

c

d

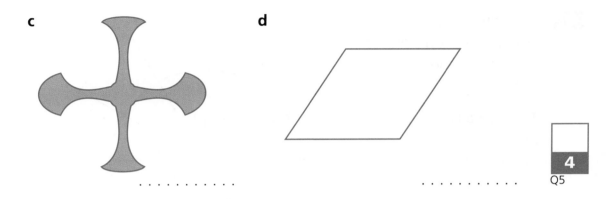

. . . .

<table>
<tr><td>4</td></tr>
</table>

Q5

Q6 **a** Reflect each group of lines in the mirror line given to make a pattern.

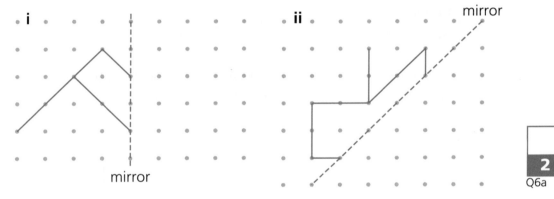

<table>
<tr><td>2</td></tr>
</table>

Q6a

  b Now use two mirror lines to make a pattern.
First reflect the group of lines in one mirror line, then reflect the whole pattern in the other mirror line.

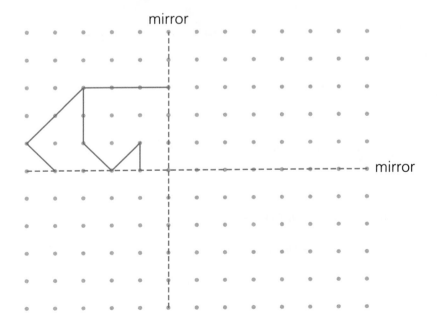

<table>
<tr><td>2</td></tr>
</table>

Q6b

Answers can be found on page 85

Q7 The British Coastguards are keeping their eyes on the foreign boats in British waters.

They see a French boat at X, this is in the direction 2 o'clock, 20 km away.

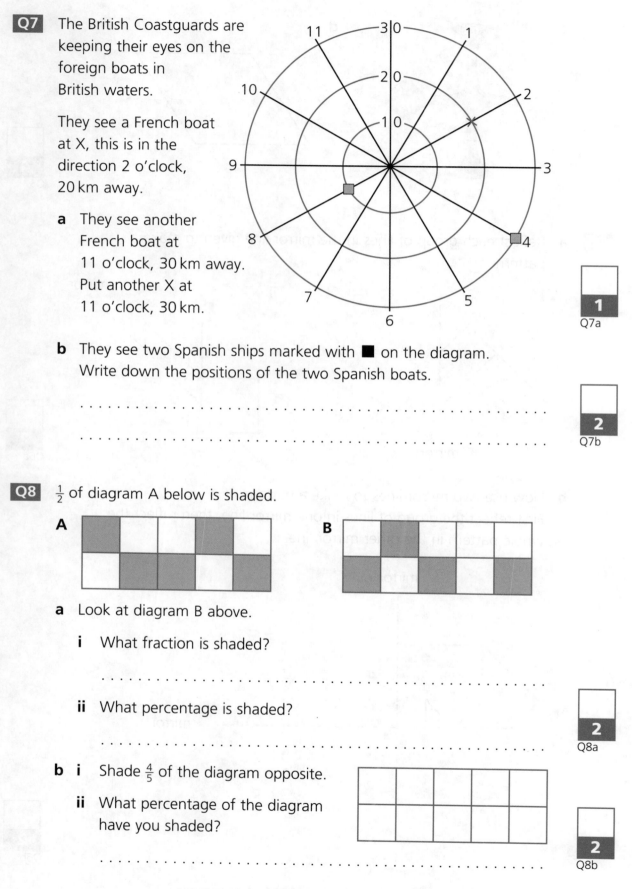

a They see another French boat at 11 o'clock, 30 km away. Put another X at 11 o'clock, 30 km.

1
Q7a

b They see two Spanish ships marked with ■ on the diagram. Write down the positions of the two Spanish boats.

. . . .

. . . .

2
Q7b

Q8 $\frac{1}{2}$ of diagram A below is shaded.

A

B

a Look at diagram B above.

i What fraction is shaded?

. . . .

ii What percentage is shaded?

. . . .

2
Q8a

b i Shade $\frac{4}{5}$ of the diagram opposite.

ii What percentage of the diagram have you shaded?

. . . .

2
Q8b

Answers can be found on pages 85–86

54

Q9 **a** Think about a survey you have done.
What did you use your survey to decide about?

. . . .

. . . .

1
Q9a

b Write down three different types of result you could get from your whole survey.

. . . .

. . . .

. . . .

. . . .

3
Q9b

Q10 Chris bought 9 packets of 'stickers' at 18 p each. He paid with a £10 note. How much change should he receive?

. . . .

. . . .

. . . .

. . . .

1
Q10

Q11 A bubble gum machine sells five different coloured balls of gum:

blue   green   yellow   orange   red

There are the same number of balls of each colour in the machine.

a Paul doesn't like the green or red balls of gum.
What is the probability that he will get a bubble gum that he likes?

. . . .

. . . .

b Amanda likes all the colours.
What is the probability that Amanda will get a bubble gum that she likes?

. . . .

. . . .

Answers can be found on page 86

c Draw an arrow on the scale to show the probability that Paul will get a sweet that he likes. Label this arrow P.

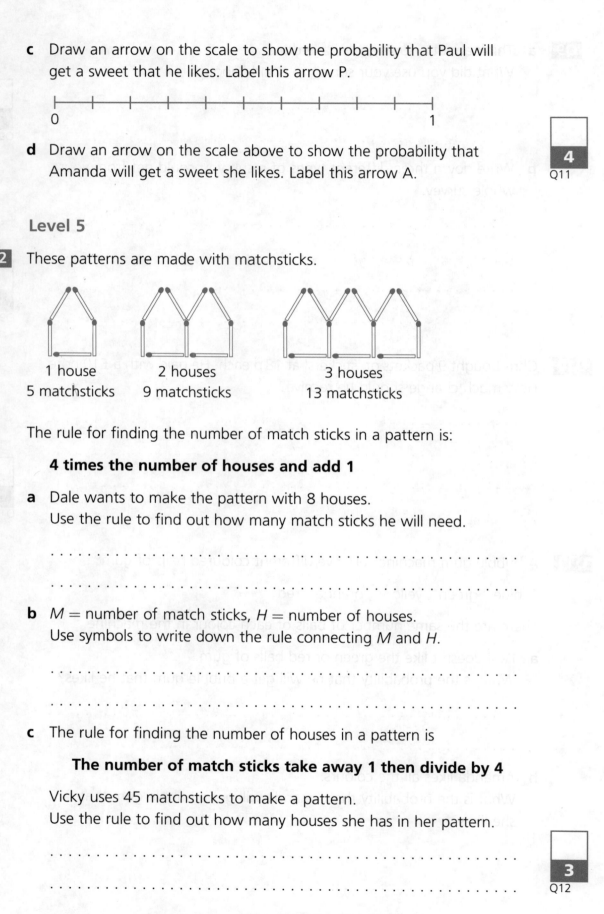

d Draw an arrow on the scale above to show the probability that Amanda will get a sweet she likes. Label this arrow A.

Level 5

Q12 These patterns are made with matchsticks.

1 house
5 matchsticks

2 houses
9 matchsticks

3 houses
13 matchsticks

The rule for finding the number of match sticks in a pattern is:

4 times the number of houses and add 1

a Dale wants to make the pattern with 8 houses.
Use the rule to find out how many match sticks he will need.

. . . .

. . . .

b M = number of match sticks, H = number of houses.
Use symbols to write down the rule connecting M and H.

. . . .

. . . .

c The rule for finding the number of houses in a pattern is

The number of match sticks take away 1 then divide by 4

Vicky uses 45 matchsticks to make a pattern.
Use the rule to find out how many houses she has in her pattern.

. . . .

. . . .

Answers can be found on page 86

Q13 There are 6 bags of sweets and 5 extra sweets.
Each bag has *n* sweets inside.

Tara says:	'There are 11*n* sweets.'
'Wayne says:	'There are 11 sweets.'
Sam says:	'There are 6*n* + 5 sweets.'
Adam says:	'There are 5 + 6 × *n* sweets.'
Peter says:	'There are 30*n* sweets.'

a Name one person who is right.

. . . .

b Name another person who is right.

. . . .

c Write down how many sweets there might have been altogether.

. . . .

. . . .

 3
Q13

Q14 Look at these numbers

    4   1   −4   10   3   −7   8   −1

a Choose one of the numbers to give the answer 7.

    3 + −4 + ... = 7

 1
Q14a

b Choose one of the numbers to give the lowest possible answer.
Fill in the space below and work out the answer.

    −1 + ... = ...

 2
Q14b

Q15 Motorists should know the smallest distance they should leave
between moving cars. These distances are different for bad weather
and good weather.

Answers can be found on page 86

This graph shows these distances.

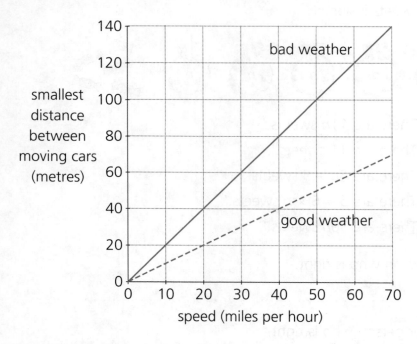

a A car is travelling at 50 miles per hour in bad weather.
What is the smallest distance it should be from the car in front?

. . . .

1 | Q15a

b A car is travelling at 65 miles per hour in good weather.
What is the smallest distance it should be from the car in front?

. . . .

1 | Q15b

c In bad weather, a car is driving 60 metres behind another car.
What is the fastest speed that this car should be travelling at?

. . . .

1 | Q15c

d You are driving at 50 miles per hour in good weather, at the
closest acceptable distance to the car in front.
The weather suddenly turns bad and you drop your speed to
40 miles per hour.
Use the graph to work out how much you need to increase the
distance between you and the car in front.

. . . .

. . . .

2 | Q15d

Answers can be found on page 86

Q16 Make an accurate full-size drawing of this triangle.

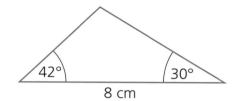

3

Q16

Q17 **a** Find the cost of 27 tickets costing 95 p each.

. . . .

. . . .

. . . .

. . . .

b How many shares priced £27 each can I buy for £650?

. . . .

. . . .

. . . .

4

Q17

. . . .

Q18 **a** Sean knows that most of the pupils in his school like to watch on TV

Neighbours   The Simpsons   Star Trek

He says: 'The probability that the first pupil I meet this morning
likes to watch *Star Trek* is $\frac{1}{3}$ because there are three programmes.'
Sean is wrong, explain why.

. . . .

. . . .

1

Q18a

. . . .

Answers can be found on page 86

b Howard came home in the rain and all the labels fell off his tins of soup.

He did remember buying 2 tins of tomato soup, 3 tins of chicken soup and 1 tin of pea soup.

He opens a tin for his tea, what is the probability that it is tomato soup?

. . . .

. . . .

2

Q18b

Answers can be found on page 86

Test B

Paper 1 With a calculator (Time: 1 hour)

Tips before you start:

- You *can* use your calculator in this paper, so do use it where you need to.
- If the question says 'calculate', then it expects you to use your calculator.
- 'Work out' is similar to calculate, except that you are expected to use a method for which you may not need a calculator.
- If the question says 'explain', make sure you write your explanation in clear English.
- Read each question carefully. Make sure you answer the question you have been asked and not your own.
- If a question says 'use the graph to', then do just that, do not do a separate calculation.
- Give the units to each answer that needs them, e.g. cm, m², litres, etc.
- Remember that you can earn marks for a wrong answer, but to do so you need to have shown the method you used to find your answer.
- If you find your mind goes blank on a particular question, then leave it, go on to the next question and come back to this question later.
- Answer every question on the paper as well as you can.
- Use your full time, check over your answers to find the careless mistakes that we all make.

Q1 The table shows some information about people in a club.

	Can drive a car	Cannot drive a car
males	37	4
females	17	23

a What percentage of the females can drive a car?

....

....

Answers can be found on page 87

61

b What is the ratio of non-car drivers to car drivers in the club?
Write the ratio in the form 1 : . . . . .

. . . .

. . . .

. . . .

c One member is chosen at random from the whole club.
What is the probability that the member chosen is a female who
can drive a car?

. . . .

. . . .

3
Q1

Q2 Three people play a game.
Each person starts the game with a bag of marbles. Each bag has
M marbles in it.
The table shows what happened during the game.

	Started with	*During the game*	*Ended the game with*
Joy	3 bags	won 3 marbles	$3M + 3$
Michael	2 bags	won 10 marbles	$2M + 10$
Brett	5 bags	lost 13 marbles	$5M - 13$

a At the end of the game, Joy and Brett had the same number of
marbles.
Write an equation to show this.

. . . .

. . . .

1
Q2a

b Solve this equation to find M, the number of marbles in each bag
at the start of the game.

. . . .

. . . .

. . . .

. . . .

2
Q2b

Answers can be found on page 87

Q3 Rachel is investigating areas and perimeters of shapes.
She makes a square with a perimeter of 20 cm.

a Calculate the area of the square.

. . . .

. . . .

b Rachel makes a rectangle with a perimeter of 20 cm.
The length is four times bigger than the width.
Calculate the area of the rectangle.

. . . .

. . . .

. . . .

. . . .

c Rachel makes a different rectangle with an area of 27 cm^2.
The sides of Rachel's rectangle are x cm and $(x + 2)$ cm.

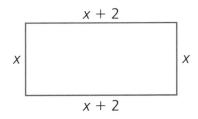

She wants to find a value of x so that $x(x + 2) = 27$.
Between which 1 decimal place numbers does x lie? Use the table below.

x	$x + 2$	area	
3	5	15	too small

6

Q3

Answers can be found on page 87

Q4 Calculate the area of this triangle.

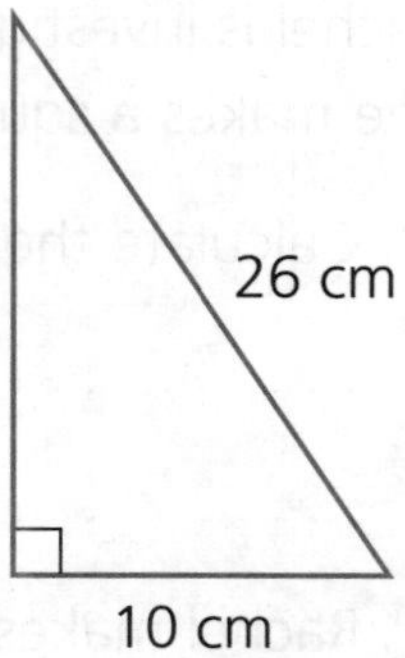

. . . .

. . . .

. . . .

. . . .

. . . .

26 cm

10 cm

3
Q4

Q5 An outdoor paddling pool was being filled with water.
The graph below shows the depth of water in the paddling pool.

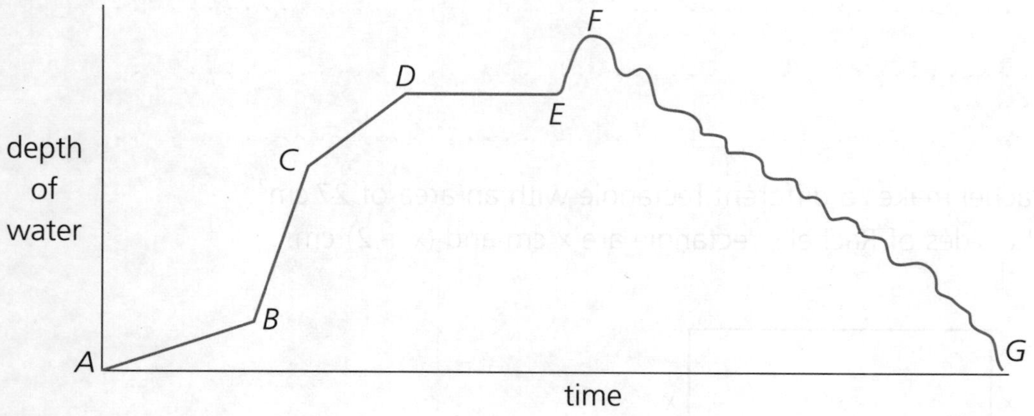

depth
of
water

time

A *B* *C* *D* *E* *F* *G*

a Explain what might be happening at point *B*.

. . . .

. . . .

. . . .

b Which part of the graph shows the paddling pool ready for the
children to start playing in it?

. . . .

c Explain what is happening from *F* to *G*.

. . . .

. . . .

. . . .

. . . .

3
Q5

Answers can be found on page 87

Q6 John wanted to find out why people in different countries grow particularly tall or remain small. He picked 16 countries and found out:

> the average height
> the average temperature
> the population

He plotted these scatter graphs to help him look for links.
Each cross stands for a country.

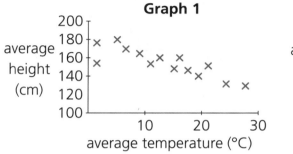

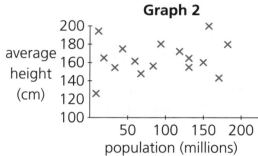

Look at the different ways in which the points in the two graphs are scattered.

a What does graph 1 show about any possible links between the average height and the average temperature in a country?

. . . .

. . . .

. . . .

b What does graph 2 show about any possible links between the average height and a country's population?

. . . .

. . . .

. . . .

John finds out two facts about the country Bantaland:

> the population is about 30 million
> the average temperature is about 22 °C

c John wants to find out the average height of this population. He is going to use one of the graphs to estimate it. Which of the two graphs is the better one for John to use?

. . . .

Answers can be found on page 87

d Use the graph to estimate the average height in Bantaland.

. . . .

. . . .

4
Q6

Q7 Derek wants to spin this spinner.
He estimated the probability of
spinning each colour as:

Black 30%   White 25%
Blue 20%   Purple 15%

How can you tell whether the total
of his probabilities is correct?

. . . .

. . . .

. . . .

1
Q7

Q8 A shoe shop had a closing down sale.
The sale started on Monday and finished on Friday.
For each day of the sale, the prices were reduced by 20% of the prices
on the day before.

a A pair of boots was priced at £24 on the Sunday, and Dale bought
them on Tuesday. How much did he pay for them?

. . . .

. . . .

. . . .

. . . .

2
Q8a

b Barbara bought a pair of sandals on the Wednesday for £8.40.
What was the price of the sandals on Tuesday?

. . . .

. . . .

. . . .

. . . .

1
Q8b

Answers can be found on page 87

Q9 Two young mathematicians were playing a number game.

Brian said: 'Multiplying my number by 5 and then subtracting 8 gives the same answer as multiplying my number by 3 and adding 2.'

a Susan called Brian's number x and formed an equation

$5x - 8 = 3x + 2$

Solve this equation and write down the value of x.

. . . .

. . . .

. . . .

Q9a

b Susan said: 'Multiplying my number by 3 and subtracting 5 gives the same answer as subtracting my number from 11.'
Call Susan's number t and form an equation.

. . . .

Q9b

c Work out the value of Susan's number.

. . . .

. . . .

. . . .

Q9c

d Martin thought of two numbers which he called m and p.
He wrote down two equations that fitted his numbers:

$m + 2p = 17$
$2m + 3p = 27$

Work out the values of m and p.

. . . .

. . . .

. . . .

. . . .

. . . .

. . . .

2

. . . .

Q9d

Answers can be found on page 87

Q10 The old style sardine tins were shaped as in the diagram opposite. Each tin had an inside depth of 4 cm.

4 cm

SARDINES

a The area of the lid was 65 cm² . Calculate the volume of sardines that the tin contained.

. . . .

. . . .

. . . .

1
Q10a

b The label that went all the way round the tin overlapped by 1 cm. The area of the label was 140 cm².

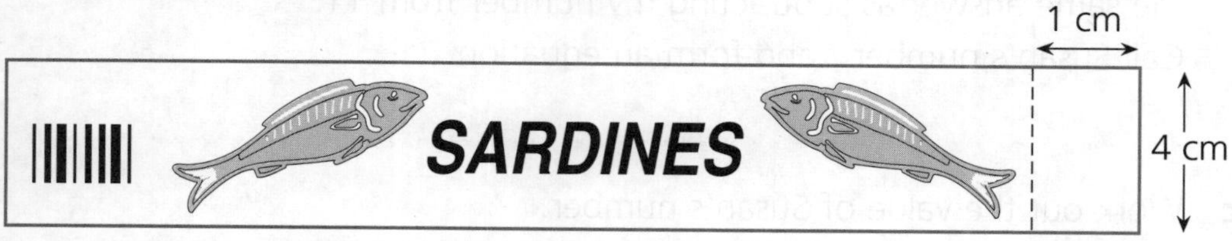

1 cm

SARDINES

4 cm

Work out the distance around the tin.

. . . .

. . . .

. . . .

2
Q10b

c The new style sardine cans are cylindrical as shown.

Does the new tin hold more or less than the old style tin? You must show all your working.

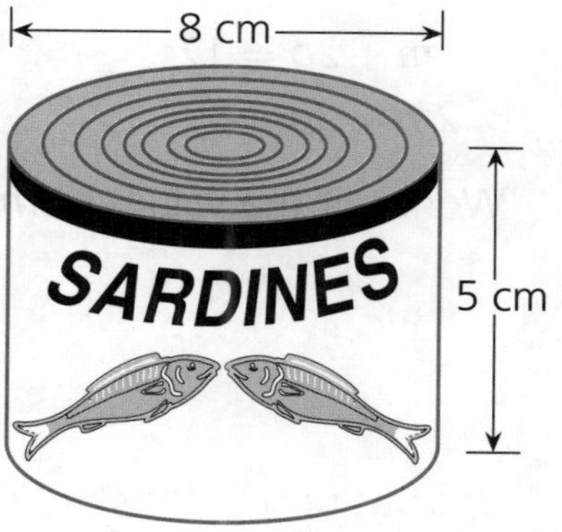

8 cm

SARDINES

5 cm

. . . .

. . . .

. . . .

. . . .

. . . .

2
Q10c

Answers can be found on page 88

Q11 A plane flies from Arcourt
to Battington.
Battington is 16 km to
the east and 12 km to
the north of Arcourt.

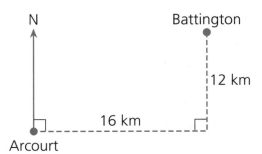

N   Battington

12 km

16 km

Arcourt

a Calculate the shortest distance between Arcourt and Battington.
Give your answer to 1 decimal place.

. . . .

. . . .

. . . .

. . . .

2
Q11a

b Calculate the bearing of Battington from Arcourt.

. . . .

. . . .

. . . .

. . . .

3
Q11b

Q12 A new sweet is put on the market, Jelly Families.
Each packet contains jelly babies and jelly parents.
A survey was made on a sample of 100 packets of Jelly Families and
the results plotted on two charts.

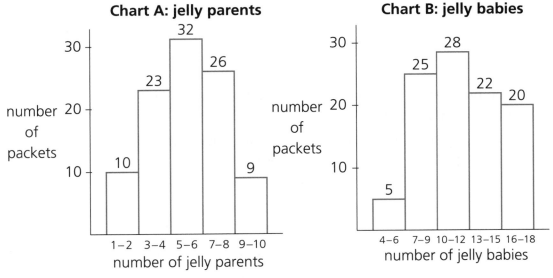

Chart A: jelly parents

32

30

26

23

number 20
of
packets

10

10

9

1–2 3–4 5–6 7–8 9–10
number of jelly parents

Chart B: jelly babies

28

30

25

22

20

number 20
of
packets

10

5

4–6 7–9 10–12 13–15 16–18
number of jelly babies

Answers can be found on page 88

a Use the table opposite to help you calculate an estimate of the mean number of jelly babies in a packet.

Number of jelly babies	Mid-point of range (x)	Number of packets (f)	fx
4–6	5	5	
7–9	8	25	
10–12	11	28	
13–15	14	22	
16–18	17	20	
		100	

. . . .

. . . .

3

Q12a

b Calculate an estimate of the number of packets that contain 6 or more jelly parents.

. . . .

. . . .

. . . .

1

Q12b

c Which of the two charts, A or B, shows the greater range?

. . . .

1

Q12c

d A packet of Jelly Families is chosen at random.
Calculate the probability that it contains fewer than 10 jelly babies.

. . . .

. . . .

. . . .

1

Q12d

e The number of jelly parents in a packet is independent of the number of jelly babies in the packet.
Calculate the probability that any packet bought at random contains 10–12 jelly babies and 5–6 jelly parents.

. . . .

. . . .

. . . .

2

Q12e

Answers can be found on page 88

Paper 2 Without a calculator (Time: 1 hour)

Tips before you start:

- You *cannot* use your calculator in this paper, so be prepared for those questions where you need to make the calculations yourself.

- If the question says 'calculate', then it expects you to use your calculator.

- If the question says 'explain', make sure you write your explanation in clear English.

- Read each question carefully. Make sure you answer the question you have been asked and not your own.

- Remember that you can earn marks for a wrong answer, but to do so you need to have shown the method you used to find your answer.

- If you find your mind goes blank on a particular question, then leave it, go on to the next question and come back to this question later.

- Answer every question on the paper as well as you can.

- Use your full time, check over your answers to find the careless mistakes that we all make.

Q1 Look at these numbers:

$$+2 \quad -7 \quad 0 \quad +8 \quad -3 \quad +5 \quad -1 \quad +1$$

a Choose one of these numbers to complete the following sum to give the lowest possible answer.

$$-3 - \ldots \ldots = \ldots \ldots$$

2
Q1a

b Choose one of the numbers given to complete the following sum to give the highest possible answer.

$$-1 - \ldots \ldots = \ldots \ldots$$

2
Q1b

Q2 The contents of a block are made by adding the two blocks underneath it.

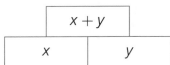

Answers can be found on page 88

a Write an expression for the top block in the following.
Write your expression as simply as possible.

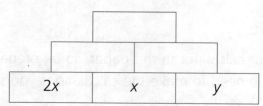

| 2x | x | y |

2
Q2a

b Fill in the missing expressions in these blocks.
Write your expression as simply as possible.

i

4x + 3

| x + 3 | x | x |

2
Q2bi

ii

4x + y

| | x | −2y |

3
Q2bii

Q3 This is a series of patterns with coloured and white bricks.

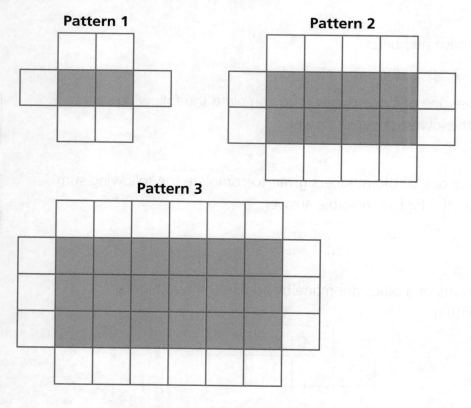

Pattern 1

Pattern 2

Pattern 3

Answers can be found on page 88

72

a How many coloured bricks and white bricks will there be in pattern 4?

. . . .

2 Q3a

b How many coloured bricks and white bricks will there be in pattern 10?

. . . .

. . . .

2 Q3b

c How many coloured bricks and white bricks will there be in pattern *n* ?

. . . .

. . . .

2 Q3c

d B = total number of bricks in a pattern, n = pattern number.
Use symbols to write down an equation connecting B and n.

. . . .

. . . .

. . . .

1 Q3d

Q4 The shape X is a square.

The instructions to draw shape X are:

FORWARD 3
TURN RIGHT 90
FORWARD 3
TURN RIGHT 90
FORWARD 3
TURN RIGHT 90
FORWARD 3

a Write instructions to draw a triangle that has sides of length 5 units.

. . . .

. . . .

. . . .

. . . .

. . . .

2 Q4a

Answers can be found on pages 84–89

b Shape Y is a parallelogram.

Complete the instructions to draw shape Y.

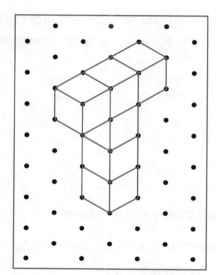

82°   7   98°

2   Y

Start

FORWARD 2

. . . .

. . . .

. . . .

2

Q4b

Q5 Tina drew a solid letter T on an isometric grid using 6 cubes.

She didn't draw any edge she couldn't see.

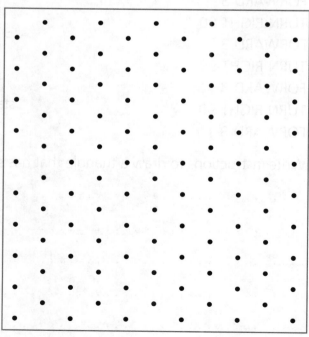

a Tina turned the T upside down.

Draw on the isometric grid here what the solid looks like.

1

Q5a

Answers can be found on page 89

b Tina wants to draw solid letters in a row so that they make her initials TE.
Complete TE on the isometric grid below (use any number of cubes).

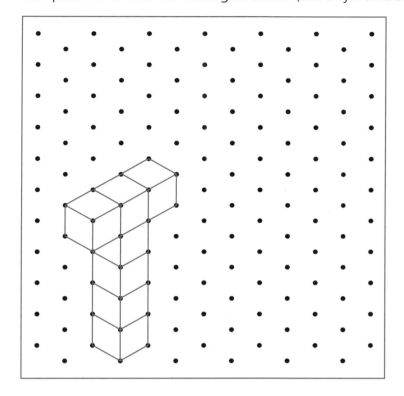

2
Q5b

Q6 Joe, Ed, Kim and Richard are the named players in a penalty shoot-out.
To decide in which order they take the penalties, all four names go
into a hat. Each name is taken out of the bag, one at a time.

a Write down all the possible orders with Joe taking the second penalty.

. . . .

. . . .

. . . .

. . . .

. . . .

. . . .

2
Q6a

b When Joe takes a penalty, the probability that he scores is $\frac{5}{8}$.
What is the probability that Joe does not score when he takes a penalty?

. . . .

. . . .

1
Q6b

Answers can be found on pages 89–90

Q7 Some students wanted to find out if the local residents wanted a new supermarket close to their village.

a One question was:

How old are you (years)?

☐ ☐ ☐ ☐ ☐

15 or younger   15 to 25   25 to 35   35 to 45   over 45

Douglas said: 'Some of these numbers must be wrong!'
Explain why Douglas is right.

. . . .

. . . .

. . . .

1
Q7a

b A different question was:

How much do you spend each week on food?

☐ ☐ ☐ ☐

nothing   not much   quite a lot   too much

Douglas said: 'But these labels are no good.'
Write new labels for these boxes.

. . . .

. . . .

. . . .

2
Q7b

The students decide to give the questionnaire to 100 people.
Helen said: 'We'll ask the pupils in our school.'

c Give one advantage of Helen's suggestion.

. . . .

. . . .

. . . .

1
Q7c

Answers can be found on page 90

76

d Give one disadvantage of Helen's suggestion.

. . . .

. . . .

. . . .

. . . .

1

Q7d

Q8 A company made wire. The diameter of its copper wire was 0.025 cm, and the diameter of its steel wire was 0.009 cm.

a What is the difference between the diameters of the two types of wire?
Give your answer in millimetres.

. . . .

. . . .

. . . .

1

Q8a

b The steel wire was wrapped around a wooden bobbin, with an available core to wrap around of length 4 cm. To cover the wooden core, how many times will the wire wrap around it?

. . . .

. . . .

. . . .

. . . .

1

Q8b

c The weight of the bobbin was given as 97.4 grams measured to the nearest tenth of a gram.
Between what two values does the weight of the bobbin actually lie?

. . . .

. . . .

. . . .

2

Q8c

Answers can be found on page 90

Q9 A teacher has some 'algebra flash cards'.

| x^2 | $0.3x$ | $\dfrac{x}{5}$ | $\sqrt{x}$ | $\dfrac{1}{x}$ |

The answers given by these cards is to be a positive number.

a Which cards will always give an answer less than x?

....

....

2
Q9a

b When x is 1, which cards will give an answer of 1 also?

....

....

2
Q9b

c When x is 5, which cards give an answer less than 5?

....

....

2
Q9c

d When x is less than 1, which cards give an answer bigger than x?

....

....

....

1
Q9d

Q10 A solid wooden ramp is in the shape of a prism.

←1 metre→   1 metre

1.6 metres

←——— 3 metres ———→

The shaded face of the ramp is a trapezium.

a Calculate the area of the shaded face.

....

....

....

....

1
Q10a

Answers can be found on page 90

b Calculate the volume of the ramp.

. . . .

. . . .

. . . .

. . . .

2
Q10b

Q11 Rebecca was investigating straight lines and their equations.
She drew these lines.

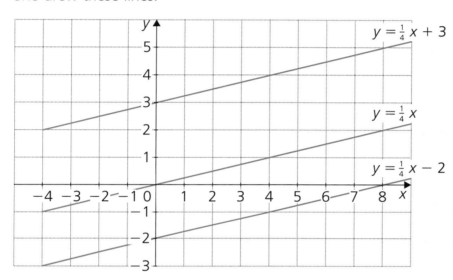

a $y = \frac{1}{4}x$ is in each equation.
Write down one fact this tells you about all the lines.

. . . .

. . . .

b The lines cross the y-axis at $(0, -2)$, $(0, 0)$ and $(0, 3)$
Which part of each equation helps you to see where the line
crosses the y-axis?

. . . .

. . . .

c Where would the line $y = \frac{1}{4}x + 25$ cross the y-axis?

. . . .

. . . .

4
Q11

d Draw on the graph the line $y = \frac{1}{4}x - 1$.

Answers can be found on page 90

79

Q12 Stan collects the eggs from hens each morning on his parents' farm. One day he counts how many eggs the producing hens have laid. These are his results for the week.

Number of eggs laid	Number of hens
1	14
2	31
3	24
4	18
5	13

a From the table state:

the mode . . . .

the median . . . .

b Calculate the mean number of eggs each producing hen has produced.

. . . .

. . . .

. . . .

. . . .

c Stan's neighbour, who has the same breed of hen, had 50 hens. Assume that on any day only 80% of the hens are producing hens. Calculate how many eggs Stan's neighbour should expect to collect each morning.

. . . .

. . . .

. . . .

. . . .

6

Q12

Answers can be found on page 90

Q13 Philip does an experiment to find out the probability of a slice of bread landing buttered side up.

He threw a slice of bread in the air 100 times and recorded the number of times it landed buttered side up.

These are the results he got at each stage in the experiment.

Number of times the bread landed butter side up	Throws so far	Estimate of probability
7	20	0.35
13	40	0.325
19	60	0.317
25	80	0.3125
31	100	0.31

a Use Philip's results to give a good estimate of the probability that a slice of buttered bread will land butter side up.

. . . .

Q13a · 1

b David also did this experiment, but he threw a slice of bread in the air 200 times. Whose results will give the better estimate of the probability? Explain why.

. . . .

. . . .

. . . .

. . . .

Q13b · 1

Answers can be found on page 90

Answers: Test A

Paper 1 With a calculator

Q1 One mark for each correct shape.

a

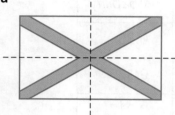

b

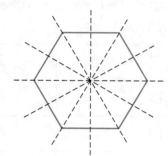

c

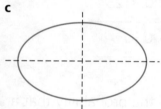

d

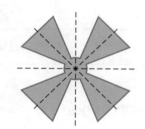

`4`

Q2 **a** $3 \times 4 = 12$ lions

b $2.5 \times 4 = 10$ chimps

c Because the last drawing is only $\frac{1}{4}$ and not $\frac{1}{2}$ of a box.

d You should show $1\frac{1}{2}$ boxes with a full giraffe in the full box and only half a giraffe in the half-box.

(1 mark for each part)

`4`

Q3 **a** London and Sheffield   **b** 140 miles   **c** $140 + 60 = 200$ miles

`3`

Q4 **a** 14   **b** 109   **c** 10   **d** 102   **e** 68

(1 mark for each correct answer)

`5`

Q5 **a** 18 cm

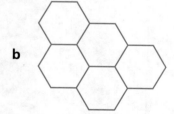

b (Will have a perimeter of 16 cm)

c (Will have a perimeter of 22 cm)

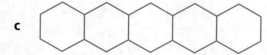

d The smallest perimeter is when the shape is all squashed close together. The largest perimeter is when the shape is spread out in a line.
(1 mark for each part)

`4`

Q6 **a** The *x* number is always the same as the *y* number.
b (15, 15)
c (11, 9)
d *A* can have any value larger than 20.
(1 mark for each part)

`4`

Q7 **a** Multiply by 3 each time.

`1`

b The following are three examples of what you might have done, but of course there are lots of possible correct answers. As long as your rule works and includes the 1, you will gain a mark. For example,
i $1 \rightarrow 4 \rightarrow 7 \rightarrow 11 \rightarrow 14$,   add 3 on each time
ii $1 \rightarrow 4 \rightarrow 16 \rightarrow 64 \rightarrow 256$,   times by 4 each time
iii $1 \rightarrow 4 \rightarrow 8 \rightarrow 13 \rightarrow 19$,   add on 3 then 4 then 5, etc.

`3`

Q8 **a** Each division represent 2 cm, so the length is 26 cm.
b Each division represent 0.1 kg, so the weight is 2.7 kg.
c 109 cm.
(1 mark for each part)

`3`

Q9 **a** C and D are the ones that will not work.
b You should show that in C, the top is on the side, so it has no lid. You should show that D has the ends at the same end, so one end is open. You score 1 mark for each net correctly shown to be wrong.
(2 marks for each part)

`4`

Q10 **a** Thompson: mean $= 40 \div 5 = 8$ minutes
                        range $= 9 - 7 = 2$ minutes
(1 mark each for the mean and the range)
Coachline: mean $= 37 \div 5 = 7.4$ minutes
                        range $= 17 - 1 = 16$ minutes
(1 mark each for the mean and the range)

`4`

b You can actually choose either bus, but whichever you choose you need to put a reason from the statistics to your choice. For example:
Thompson because it had a smaller range, or Coachline because it had a lower mean.

`1`

Q11 a

	3	5	7
6	3	1	1
8	5	3	1
9	6	4	2

You score 1 mark for indicating all 9 combinations (this could be just in a list), and you score 1 mark for indicating correctly what all the differences are.

2

b $\frac{6}{9}$

1

c $\frac{7}{9}$

1

Q12

	Width	Length
rectangle Q	3	5
rectangle R	9	14
rectangle S	27	41

(1 mark each correct pair)

3

Q13 a $2t + p$ **b** $5m + 2q + 3$ **c** $4m + 4$
(1 mark for each part)

3

Q14 a You could have chosen any set from (1, 3, 3), (3, 3, 5), (3, 9, 10) or (5, 9, 10).

b Any other set not included in the list above will do.

c Because the two smaller sides don't add up to more than the longest.
(1 mark for each part)

3

Q15 a Add all the heights to get to 30 days.

1

b Month A has more sunshine than month B. Month B has 1 more day than month A.

2

Q16 a 4, 9, 16, 25 (Note for every error or omission 1 mark is lost)

b 7, 11, 23 (Again, every error or omission will lose 1 mark)
(2 marks for each part)

4

Q17 a £N **b** £$3N$ **c** £$(N + 10)$ **d** £$(6N + 10)$
(You would not lose any marks anywhere in this question just because you left out your £ sign. 1 mark for each part)

4

Q18 a 1 pound (lb), 450 grams

b 3 litres, 5.3 pints
(1 mark for each correct unit)

4

The total for the paper is 68 marks.
- To gain a Level 3 you should have scored 20 marks or over.
- To gain a Level 4 you should have scored 40 marks or over.
- To gain a Level 5 you should have scored 55 marks or over.

Paper 2 Without a calculator

Q1 **a** Correct arrow on 32 °C
  b Correct arrow on −7 °C
  c 3 °C (could be indicated on the thermometer)
  d −6, −3, 1, 4, 15   (1 mark for each part)   `4`

Q2 **a** £3.20   `1`
  b Long multiplication is needed to get to £95.20.   `2`
  c Long division is needed to get to 9 people, or you could use trial and improvement since you can see that the answer is under 10.   `2`

Q3 **a** 8   **b** $\frac{1}{4}$ (1 mark each part)   `2`
  c 24 − (6 + your answer to part **a**) = 10   `2`

Q4 **a** White, because she has more white than blue.
  b Robert's, because he has more whites per blue than Donna.
  c Your arrow should be between 0 and Donna's arrow.
  d 1 out of 3, which should be written as $\frac{1}{3}$.
  e Your arrow should be between Donna's and the halfway mark.
  (1 mark for each part)   `5`

Q5 **a** 4   **b** 6   **c** 2   **d** 2
  (1 mark for each part)   `4`

Q6 **a** One mark for drawing the correct reflection on both figures, see below.

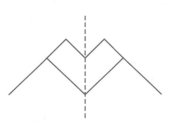 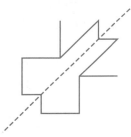   `2`

  b One mark for reflecting the group of lines in one mirror line, and one mark for correctly reflecting the whole pattern in the other mirror line, see opposite.

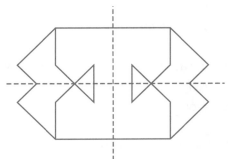   `2`

Q7 **a** One mark for correctly putting an X on 11 o'clock, 30 km.   `1`
  b (8, 10) and (4, 30)
  (1 mark for each correct position identified)   `2`

Q8 **a** **i** $\frac{4}{10}$ **ii** 40%   `2`

b **i** 8 small squares should have been shaded in **ii** 80%   `2`

Q9 **a** Anything plausible will earn you 1 mark.   `1`

b As long as your results were possible you would get 1 mark for each.   `3`

Q10 You work out 9 × 18 p to get £1.62, then take this away from £10 to get £8.38   `1`

Q11 **a** $\frac{3}{5}$ **b** $\frac{5}{5}$ or 1   (1 mark for each part)

c and **d** One mark for each correct arrow, see below.

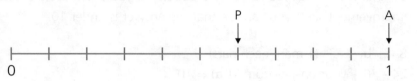

`4`

Q12 **a** 33   **b** $M = 4H + 1$ **c** 11

(1 mark for each part)   `3`

Q13 **a** Sam or Adam   **b** The name you didn't use in part **a**

c 11 or 17 or 23 or 29 or 35 (or any multiple of 6, minus 1)

(1 mark for each part)   `3`

Q14 **a** 8   `1`

b −7, −8   `2`

(1 mark for each of these)

Q15 **a** 100 metres   **b** 65 metres   **c** 30 mph   (1 mark for each part)   `3`

d From 50 to 80, an increase of 30 metres.   `2`

Q16 You would get 1 mark for each angle being no more than 2° out and

1 mark for the line being 8 cm to the nearest millimetre.   `3`

Q17 **a** Long multiplication to give £25.65   **b** Long division to get 24

(Note that neither the remainder nor the decimal places are wanted.

2 marks for each part)   `4`

Q18 **a** Because they are not equally likely chances, only a few might like

Neighbours for instance.   `1`

b $\frac{2}{6}$ or $\frac{1}{3}$ `2`

The total for the paper is 66 marks.

- To gain a Level 3 you should have scored 20 marks or over.
- To gain a Level 4 you should have scored 40 marks or over.
- To gain a Level 5 you should have scored 55 marks or over.

Answers: Test B

Paper 1 with a calculator

Q1 **a** $\frac{17}{40} \times 100 = 42.5\%$ (or 43%) **b** $27 : 54 = 1 : 2$ **c** $\frac{17}{81}$
(1 mark for each part)

`3`

Q2 **a** $3M + 3 = 5M - 13$
  b $16 = 2M$, hence $M = 8$

`1`

`2`

Q3 **a** One side will be 5 cm, so area is 25 cm^2
  b If width is x then length is $4x$, so perimeter is $10x$, making $x = 2$.
Dimensions are 2 cm by 8 cm, giving an area of 16 cm^2.
  c Between 4.2 and 4.3
(2 marks for each part)

`6`

Q4 You must first use Pythagoras to find the vertical height of the triangle.
height $= \sqrt{(26^2 - 10^2)} = 24$
area $= \frac{1}{2} \times 10 \times 24 = 120$ cm^2

`3`

Q5 **a** The tap was turned up or water going in faster.
  b DE.
  c The children are splashing about and so water is spilling out of the pool
and the water level is going down.
(1 mark for each part)

`3`

Q6 **a** The hotter the country the smaller the average height.
  b There is no link between average height and population.
  c Graph 1.
  d About 140 cm.
(1 mark for each part)

`4`

Q7 They should all add up to 100. Clearly his estimates are wrong!

`1`

Q8 **a** £24 $\rightarrow$ £19.20 $\rightarrow$ £15.36
  b £8.40 $\div$ 80 $\times$ 100 = £10.50

`2`

`1`

Q9 **a** $x = 5$ **b** $3t - 5 = 11 - t$ **c** $t = 4$
(1 mark for each part)
  d $m = 3$, $p = 7$

`3`

`2`

Q10 a $65 \times 4 = 260\,\text{cm}^3$ `1`

    b $140 \div 4 = 35\,\text{cm}$, but 1 cm overlap, so perimeter of tin = 34 cm.   `2`

    c New tin volume $= \pi \times 4^2 \times 5 = \pi \times 16 \times 5 = 251\,\text{cm}^3$. We see that the new tin holds less than the old one.   `2`

Q11 a Use Pythagoras: $\sqrt{(16^2 + 12^2)} = 20\,\text{km}$ `2`

    b The angle from North clockwise will be found by finding the angle in the bottom left-hand corner of the diagram and taking it away from 90. This bottom angle is found by $\tan^{-1}\left(\frac{12}{16}\right) = 37°$. Take this from 90 to give bearing of 053°   `3`

Q12 a Complete the last column in the table as: 25, 200, 308, 308, 340 giving a total of 1181. Divide this by 100 to give 11.81.   `3`

    b $9 + 26 + \frac{1}{2} \times 32 = 51$ `1`

    c B, jelly babies   `1`

    d $\frac{30}{100}$ or 0.3 or 30%   `1`

    e $0.28 \times 0.32 = 0.0896$ `2`

The total for the paper is 49 marks.
- To gain a Level 6 you should have scored 20 marks or over.
- To gain a Level 7 you should have scored 36 marks or over.

Paper 2 without a calculator

Q1 a 8, -11
      (1 mark for each)   `2`

    b $-7, 6$
      (1 mark for each)   `2`

Q2 a $4x + y$ `2`

    b **i** $2x + 3, 2x$
        (1 mark for each block correctly filled)   `2`

      ii $3x + y, x - 2y, 5x - y$
        (1 mark for each block correctly filled)   `3`

Q3 a 32 coloured and 24 white
      (1 mark for each)   `2`

    b 200 coloured and 60 white
      (1 mark for each)   `2`

    c $2n^2$ coloured bricks and $6n$ white bricks
        (1 mark for each)

`2`

    d $B = 2n^2 + 6n$

`1`

Q4 **a** FORWARD 5
         TURN RIGHT 120
         FORWARD 5
         TURN RIGHT 120
         FORWARD 5

`2`

    b RIGHT TURN 82
         FORWARD 7
         RIGHT TURN 98
         FORWARD 2
         RIGHT TURN 82
         FORWARD 7

`2`

Q5 **a**

`1`

    b

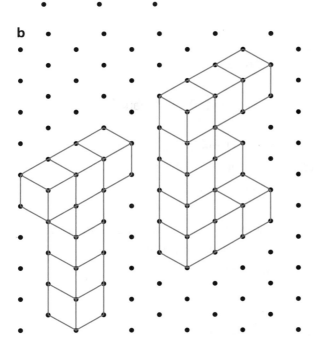

Similar answers are acceptance, e.g. using eight cubes for the letter E.

`2`

Q6 **a** EJKM   EJMK   KJEM   KJME   MJEK   MJKE | **2**

b $1 - \frac{5}{8} = \frac{3}{8}$ | **1**

Q7 **a** There is overlap in the groups, for example someone aged 25 has two boxes to choose from. | **1**

b Your labels need to be specific and cover the whole price range possibility, for example: £20 or less; over £20 but less than £40; £40 or more. | **2**

c Any answer that suggests that this is easier to do, or safer to do. | **1**

d Any answer that suggests that these students do not do the buying, or that they will not know the amounts | **1**

Q8 **a** $(0.025 - 0.009) \times 10 = 0.16\,\text{mm}$ | **1**

b $4 \div 0.009 = 444$ (accept any decimal places) | **1**

c 97.35 grams and 97.45 grams
(1 mark for each correct value) | **2**

Q9 **a** $0.3x$ and $x/5$
(1 mark each, but lose a mark for any extra ones given) | **2**

b x^2 and $1/x$ (accept $\sqrt{x}$ also)
(1 mark each, but lose a mark for any extra ones given) | **2**

c $0.3x$, $x/5$, $\sqrt{x}$ and $1/x$
(2 marks, but lose a mark for any extra ones given) | **2**

d $1/x$ and $\sqrt{x}$ | **1**

Q10 **a** $2\,\text{m}^2$ | **1**

b $2 \times 1.6 = 3.2\,\text{m}^3$ | **2**

Q11 **a** They are all parallel

b The second number in the co-ordinate

c (0, 25)

d The line should go through $(0, -1)$ and $(4, 0)$ (1 mark for each part) | **4**

Q12 **a** mode = 2 eggs, median = 3 eggs   (1 mark each)

b 285 eggs altogether divided by 100 hens = 2.85 eggs

c $0.8 \times 50 \times 2.85 = 114$ (2 marks for each part) | **6**

Q13 **a** The most accurate will be the one with most results taken into account, which is the last one, hence the best estimate is 0.31 | **1**

b David's will because he has done more trials. | **1**

The total for the paper is 59 marks.
- To gain a Level 6 you should have scored 24 marks or over.
- To gain a Level 7 you should have scored 45 marks or over.

Marking Grid – Test A

Paper 1 (pages 39–49)

Question	Marks available	Marks scored
1	4	
2	4	
3	3	
4	5	
5	4	
6	4	
7	4	
8	3	
9	4	
10	5	
11	4	
12	3	
13	3	
14	3	
15	3	
16	4	
17	4	
18	4	
total	68	

Paper 2 (pages 50–60)

Question	Marks available	Marks scored
1	4	
2	5	
3	4	
4	5	
5	4	
6	4	
7	3	
8	4	
9	4	
10	1	
11	4	
12	3	
13	3	
14	3	
15	5	
16	3	
17	4	
18	3	
total	66	

Using the marking grid

	Test 1	Test 2	Test 1+2
Maximum mark	68	66	134
Level 3	20+	20+	40+
Level 4	40+	40+	80+
Level 5	55+	55+	110+

Mark scored in Test 1 [＿＿] ▶ level [＿＿]

Mark scored in Test 2 [＿＿] ▶ level [＿＿]

Total [＿＿] ▶ level [＿＿]

Marking Grid – Test B

Paper 1 (pages 61–70)

Question	Marks available	Marks scored
1	3	
2	3	
3	6	
4	3	
5	3	
6	4	
7	1	
8	3	
9	5	
10	5	
11	5	
12	8	
total	**49**	

Paper 2 (pages 71–81)

Question	Marks available	Marks scored
1	4	
2	7	
3	7	
4	4	
5	3	
6	3	
7	5	
8	4	
9	7	
10	3	
11	4	
12	6	
13	2	
total	**59**	

Using the marking grid

	Test 1	Test 2	Test 1+2
Maximum mark	49	59	108
Level 6	20+	24+	44+
Level 7 or above	36+	45+	81+

Mark scored in Test 1 [ ] ▶ level [ ]

Mark scored in Test 2 [ ] ▶ level [ ]

Total [ ] ▶ level [ ]